Amazon Ads for Authors

Tips and Strategies to Sell Your Books

Deb Potter

Published by:
The Fairytale Factory Ltd.
Wellington,
New Zealand.

ISBN: 9781079167207

DEB POTTER

AMAZON ADS FOR AUTHORS

Table of Contents

1. Introduction

Amazon Advertising works. It sells my books. Understanding how to make money from my ads was a steep expensive learning curve. Here is the book I wish I had when I started my journey into Amazon Advertising.

Those of us who published before we could advertise on Amazon will probably never stop thanking our lucky stars that we can now advertise right where people go to buy or borrow our books.

Amazon is the best marketplace authors have ever had to connect with readers, but, as I write this, there are over 70 million books on Amazon with 70k more being published each month. You can to sell a book almost anywhere in the world through Amazon, but it can still be difficult to connect your book to your potential readers. I used to fantasize about getting my books in front of readers *looking for books like mine.* And then one day I could. And then I could advertise in England, and then Germany, and then even more countries.

Amazon ads have improved my sales. But that's not all. They have also helped me understand my readership.

The reason I sell lots of books using Amazon ads is that I have a strategy. I make relevant keyword ads, filtering in potential readers and filtering out those who do not respond to my brand. I test my existing categories and experiment with new categories. I monitor, analyze, and optimize. I create relevant ads that Amazon wants to serve.

I've made mistakes, some very painful in the pocket. I'll tell you about those, and how I learned from them, so you don't have to.

Before you start advertising, ask yourself about the quality of your books. Does your book have a great cover that fits its genre? Is your book conforming to reader expectations? Is your book well edited and proofed? If your answer is 'no' to any of those questions, then editing, proofing and covers are where you should be spending your money.

However, if you have a good quality product and an idea of who might want to read it, let's get making ads to sell more of your books!

I published my first book in 2012. I didn't sell many books but I learned about the process of writing a book, getting critical feedback, hiring an editor, commissioning a cover, and finally, publishing a book. In 2013 I published a few more books. I thought that because I'd published more books in the same genre, and by improving what I'd produced, I'd get more sales. And sales did go up … but not by much. It didn't help that my books were in a tiny niche.

I did a lot better in 2014 and 2015. I had a good share of my market and I began selling paperbacks to compliment the eBooks. At this stage I was pretty happy. People said if I picked a better selling genre I could sell more, but … I like writing what I feel like writing.

In 2016 I started advertising through (Kindle Direct Publishing) KDP. I had tried a few things outside of Amazon with limited success and, more often, failure. Then along came the chance to advertise eBooks through KDP, Amazon's platform for indie-publishers and small presses like mine. By this time, I had several authors writing for my middle grade brand, and I felt pressure to sell more of *their* books. I immediately got burned with Amazon Advertising. But I stayed in, and started experimenting. I started selling a lot more books. Because of my success, author friends asked me for help with their ads.

So, I did a few Skype and FaceTime sessions and the occasional workshop. When you have to explain things to others you get a deeper understanding yourself. Did I mention I live in New Zealand? I did a lot of teaching at crazy times of day and night. I made notes for my first pupils and photographed them for authors I swap notes with.

A year later I saw my notes in a Facebook group I'd joined—the same photographs with my handwriting. I was pleased my notes were useful, but I'd learned more since then, and Amazon has been evolving, so these are my improved notes, first published in 2019 and now revised for 2020.

I thoroughly enjoy playing with Amazon Advertising and I hope this primer gets you into the fun zone too. Let's get into it.

2. Acronyms, Terms and Concepts

These are important terms and concepts to understand. I've put them at the front so you can find them easily, and so you know they are here.

ACOS Advertising Cost of Sale, or: a metric on your advertising reports you should treat with extreme caution. It includes third party purchases (for which you receive lower royalties) and does not include page read revenue (for those in KDP). Sales can be counted up to 14 days after a click *including sales of your other titles.*

ACPC Average Cost Per Click. An *estimate* of the average amount spent to show your ad. It's calculated by adding the cost of each click and dividing by however many clicks you've had. If you haven't had many clicks the average is less meaningful as it works best over a long array. Your average will become less meaningful if you change your bid or your daily budget. For this reason, some people never change their bids, they just make new ads. I am not one of those people.

Ad blocking is software or other tools used to block ads, such as yours! If you are running ad blockers you won't be able to read your ad blurbs in your KDP account and you won't see your ads running on Amazon. Hint: Switch off your ad blockers if you want to understand Amazon advertising.

Ad copy (or **ad blurb**) is the written advertising copy that supports your ads, particularly the ads that sit under the landing pages of other books. Writers typically obsess over their 'book blurb', which is the copy supporting a book on its landing page.

Ad groups let you share targets and keywords over multiple ads.

Adjacent market is a readership that isn't an exact fit, but might turn out to love your work. You can use ads to try and lure them to your stories.

Algorithm An automated set of rules that is never as smart as we'd all like. Amazon uses more than one. Algorithms are usually simpler than people imagine.

Also-boughts are found on product pages. They are carousels of titles that customers have bought who also bought that title. They help customers find other books they'd like based on sales history. They also help you understand your readership.

Also-viewed A lower order of also-bought, often found under books or products which are selling lower volumes or just building their profile. Amazon plays with also-viewed all the time.

Amazon Ads Advertising you run on Amazon pages. Accounts are country-specific. Authors most commonly use the advertising service on the Kindle Direct Platform (KDP), but you can also set up advertising accounts through Seller Central.

Amazon Advantage A wider Amazon advertising platform for sellers with non-book products. Some authors gained accounts during 2017/18 to advertise books in other Amazon stores. In 2019 Amazon broadened the Amazon Ads platform bringing in much of the Advantage functionality. You aren't missing out on much if you don't have one.

Bid The highest value you are prepared to pay for a click on your ad.

Buy box The buy box is the yellow box on the right of a product. It's the final step of the path to a buy. You cannot advertise if you do not control the buy box.

Campaign A sustained war strategy, a civil action plan (such as the campaign for women's suffrage) and, latterly, a term used by marketers to mean messages to sell stuff. Amazon uses the word 'campaign' in place of 'advertisement', presumably because you'll keep a good ad marching on and on.

Carousel A strip of sponsored ads, also-boughts, or also-viewed found under a product. Buyers will pass the carousel on the way down to read reviews. It's called a carousel because customers can hit an arrow to see more items and eventually return to the first items on display. An item needs to be visible on the carousel to count as an impression. The word carousel goes back to medieval times when knights, riding in circles, practiced various agility feats. This might explain why amusement park carousel rides often feature horses.

Click is when your ad gets clicked on. A great keyword will give you about one click per 100 impressions/views but one click per one thousand impressions is common.

CPC Cost Per Click. The average amount you are paying for a click on one of your ads. The smaller the number of clicks you have, the more volatile your CPC is.

CTR Click Through Rate. The ratio of clicks per impressions. A high CTR may mean your ad has low relevance for your keyword selection or product targeting. It may also mean a lot of your audience has ad blockers enabled.

Daily budget The total amount you are prepared to pay on an ad each day. Starting low is a good idea. Lowering your bids is even better.

IMO In My Opinion. You'll get a lot of this in the second part of this book, so just remember that YMMV.

Impression When your ad is served, meaning it shows up somewhere in front of a human being, it is called an 'impression'. Your impressions will be far higher than your number of clicks. A click through rate (CTR) is a reporting measure that compares impressions to actual clicks.

Incognito Most browsers offer a mode known as 'incognito' to give you a way to browse the internet privately. Find yours by Googling your <browser name + incognito mode> When you are in this private window you won't save search history, cookies, site data, or information entered on forms. This is handy for moving between different Amazon advertising accounts.

Keywords (or **KW**) are the bait you use to get your ads shown. They can be single words, collections of words, phrases, and also numbers. You can also use ASINs.

Keyword finders Tools that suggest keywords by using web scraping methods or mining public sources of information such as Google Search Terms. There are many free keyword finders as well as paid tools.

KDP is the acronym for the Kindle Direct Publishing platform, and you already know that.

Lockscreen ads are full screen ads that appear on some Amazon reading devices on start up.

Loss leading is a marketing strategy where the sale price doesn't recoup the seller's costs. You might set up a loss leader campaign when you have strong read through in a series or when you can offset the loss with a lot of organic sales. I don't do this.

Online calculator Tools that can help you calculate ROI and tax and other handy things.

Portfolios are groups of campaigns. You can use them to manage a budget across multiple ads. They are handy for co-authored titles.

PPC Pay Per Click is a common internet advertising model used by Amazon, Google and many more. You pay only when someone clicks an ad, not when it is delivered. You usually bid to have your ad shown.

Read through is the term used for additional reading to books 2, 3 and 4 etc. in a series.

Relevance is the desired state of your ads. It's an Amazon term, so the dictionary won't help you. Relevance is the result of a much-debated set of optimal conditions. Amazon says relevance is important to ensure good customer experience. Amazon won't show ads that are not 'relevant to the customer's search'. If our ad is relevant it may be served more often and cost you less, since Amazon anticipates profit from sales.

ROI Return On Investment. The return on your ads relative to what they cost. A negative ROI is a loss. Use an online calculator, or divide your profit by your investment. For instance, if you make $30 and you spend $10 your profit is $20 and your ROI is $20/$10 or 200 percent.

Seller You.

SEO Search Engine Optimization. A term used most often to describe optimization of web pages by the placement, for instance, of metadata and keywords.

Web scraping is harvesting data from web pages and metadata. Keyword finding tools are built using web scraping techniques. Web scraping is also known as data scraping and screen scraping. While automated web scraping can cover millions of pages and return lots of information, human beings like you and I still have to make sense of the information. We can often do a very good manual web scrape ourselves.

Wide is the term for books not in KDP Select and therefore exclusive to Amazon. They will be available on other platforms such as Kobo and Apple Books, etc.

YMMV Your mileage may vary! Keep this in mind with any advice you receive about advertising with Amazon or other platforms. Things change. The market is different from genre to genre. The market changes over time. Trust your own data first.

3. How you will be billed for Amazon advertising

Make sure you understand how billing works before you start advertising.

As an author, you'll know that Amazon pays royalties 60 days after sales for any particular month. That isn't how ad billing works. In the beginning, you'll pay for your advertising frequently and promptly. Expect to be billed for your first couple of dollars of advertising, presumably to validate your credit card, then in increments of $50, then $100. Later, once you've earned the trust of the billing algorithm, you'll get billed at the end of each month.

Advertising might become a very important part of your author business, so update your billing information when you get a new credit card and make sure it isn't overdrawn. If you default on payment *all your ads will be cancelled.* An ad that gets switched off and on will not always continue to perform, so you don't want this to happen. If you are using a debit card, keep some credit on it, especially in the first few months when Amazon will surprise you with regular small withdrawals to check you're awake and able to pay.

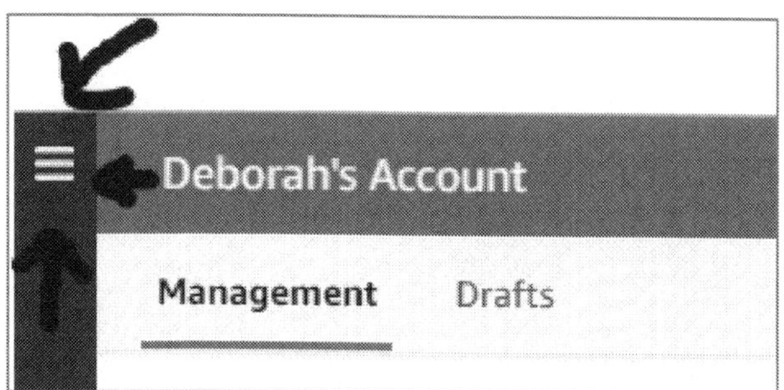

You can see your accumulating spend by clicking the three lines in the upper left corner of the main ads page, and choosing **billing and payments**. This will show you billing for the country campaigns you are currently working on. You'll more regularly see your spend on ads when you look at your ads console by 'this month'. This is a great way to keep track of spend as you go. . I keep multiple windows open for each country I advertise in.

If you have co-authored books on your account, you'll find a breakdown of spend by ad within monthly bills. You'll also see that Amazon makes adjustments when ads occasionally overspend on their budget.

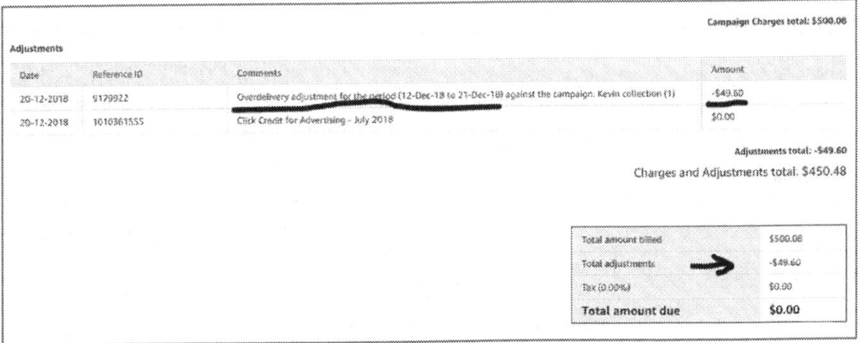

Campaign Charges total: $500.08

Adjustments

Date	Reference ID	Comments	Amount
20-12-2018	9179922	Overdelivery adjustment for the period (12-Dec-18 to 21-Dec-18) against the campaign: Kevin collection (1)	-$49.60
29-12-2018	1010361555	Click Credit for Advertising - July 2018	$0.00

Adjustments total: -$49.60

Charges and Adjustments total: $450.48

Total amount billed	$500.08
Total adjustments	-$49.60
Tax (0.00%)	$0.00
Total amount due	**$0.00**

Your accumulating bill is a canary in your advertising coal mine. If your spend shoots up, you might have accidentally bid silly money or have an automatic ad going rogue.

Amazon only keeps about 12 months billing history for you to refer back to. Make a regular habit of downloading your bills to maintain good business records.

One last thing from the Amazon fine print, and I promise to get on to sexier stuff: your campaign's 'daily budget' is actually aggregated by Amazon to a *monthly* budget. So a daily budget of $20 to you, is a monthly spend of $620 to Amazon. If your daily spend is tracking high on day 20, Amazon can (and will) fix that by reducing the serves of your ad for the rest of the month. If your ad is underspent, it could get very active toward the end of the month.

4. Where are the ads?

If you aren't seeing sponsored ads when you browse Amazon, you might be running ad blocker software. That's going to cramp your style, so I suggest you switch it off. You can run ads without seeing them (whew!) but you learn a lot by observing who is showing up under your books and who is paying to sit beside your competition.

If you are looking at Amazon pages from another country, you still might not see ads being delivered. To see the ads in the USA all the time, set a default delivery address there. I like to set my default address to one of the properties of Jeff Bezos. If I accidentally send him an author copy one day, I'll consider it a thank you for setting up a way for me to sell books around the world.

Ads aren't always blocked in other Amazon stores, for instance I see ads in the UK from my ISP in New Zealand. This is handy because the UK is my biggest market.

5. Setting up an Amazon ad

If you have a KDP account you can make ads for your books through Amazon Advertising. The ads you make for the American store will only show up on Amazon.com for American readers (and some, but not all, overseas readers with a .com account). To get ads showing up in other Amazon stores, you need to set up a separate account, also through KDP. You can't do this in every Amazon store but the United Kingdom, Germany, Italy, Spain and France were all added in 2019. Later in the book I'll give you some insights to help you navigate advertising in other countries but we'll focus on the US first.

To make a new ad, open up your KDP account and get to ads by going to your Bookshelf.

Click on Promote and Advertise to advertise an eBook. To make a paperback ad, click on the three little dots and choose Promote and Advertise. In 2018 Amazon opened up advertising to print books as well as eBooks—make sure you know which one you've selected. Many genres attract more eBook buyers than paperbacks. For instance, I sell more middle grade paperbacks than eBooks, so I tend to advertise the physical books.

Next you'll choose a marketplace.

The first time you visit the advertising page, you'll need to sign up and confirm your credit card details. I'll assume you don't need any help with that, but do check out my notes about credit cards in the chapter above and in the Tips chapter.

Once you've authorized Amazon to take your money, you'll see something like the snip below:

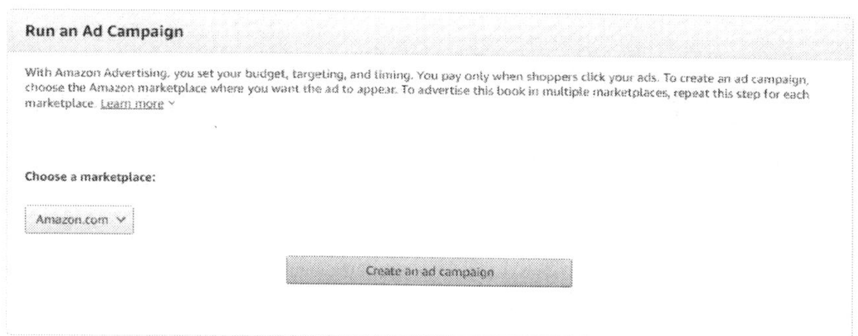

At this point you could bookmark Amazon's help pages by clicking Learn more – if you do you'll get another window open and I encourage you to open it and have a bit of a scan or leave it for later.

To make your first ad hit the yellow button currently reading Create an ad campaign (last month it read Create campaign and next month it may read differently again). Next, on Amazon US, you are invited to Choose Your Campaign Type. Your first choice is between a **Sponsored Product** and a **Lockscreen Ad.**

The Lockscreen choice gives you a full-page ad that will appear on some Amazon reading devices. That placement makes Lockscreen ads very appealing! I consider the Lockscreen ad to be quite a blunt instrument that is unsuitable for many genres. If you have money to burn, you could start with a Lockscreen ad, but I recommend you stop, wait, and learn from Sponsored Products first. Pick **Sponsored Product**.

SPONSORED PRODUCTS

Sponsored Products appear in customer searches, in carousels across the bottom of the landing pages of other books, and other places Amazon might trial from time to time. Amazon is always trying new things. Wherever the Sponsored Product ads appear, they will have a little 'sponsored ad' label on them somewhere. You'll probably start noticing these whenever you're on Amazon pages from now on.

Click on CONTINUE under the Sponsored Products option. If you can't see the CONTINUE button to start your ad, scroll down to find it.

Now we're really getting somewhere. Let's make an ad.

Step 1: Campaign name

It's easy to overlook this first box. If you ignore it, Amazon will give your ad campaign a default name. Instead, give the campaign a meaningful name. You might call it Dave or Miranda or Frances. Or, you might give it a name that 'says what's in the tin' such as '1First ad' or something like that. (I'd love to hear what you call your first ad because you're a writer, and you'll probably come up with something cool).

Later, when you start to analyze your ads, your campaign name will be useful high level information. The sorts of ideas you might want to seed into a campaign name are: the title of the book, a memory jog about the ad blurb you used, a seasonal memory jog (Xmas ad, etc.), and a clue about the targets you used or a strategy you are applying.

If you ever forget to name your ad in a meaningful way you can rename them once they are running in **Campaign settings**.

Names aren't too important right now, so let's move on to step 2.

Step 2: Start and end date

I always leave my end dates open. If the ad turns out to be a cracker I don't want it to end. You'll be able to pause or terminate ads, so I strongly suggest no end date. You *can* delay the start of an ad but generally you want them to turn on RIGHT NOW. An example of when you might choose to *delay* the launch of an ad would be when your ad blurb is seasonal "Curl up by the fire with..." or "Breeze through tax season with..." (You could name that first seasonal ad idea *Fireside ad*). If you see an option to join a portfolio just ignore this for now.

Step 3: Daily budget

This is your first ad. Let's set a conservative daily budget. Your daily budgets will get higher as you gain confidence and find out what works for your books. Go ahead and put in a number you feel comfy with. I suggest $20 for starters.

Most newbies start with daily budgets of about $5. You really don't get much for five bucks. If Amazon makes a commitment not to spend more than $5, their algorithm will manage that $5 budget by taking your ad out for a spin at 5am for ten minutes. Well, that's my theory. So a slightly higher daily budget will give your ad more chance of being delivered onto a page for someone to see.

Step 4: Targeting

If you like, Amazon will target automatically. There is a place for Auto Ads and we'll cover that in more detail later. They do much better if they draw from good information. The Amazon program is very good at showing people who are searching for toilet rolls, different toilet roll choices, and different towels to towel buyers—but books are different. An auto ad won't perform *when it currently has no information about what works.* So we make manually targeted ads, learn some stuff, and then later add a few auto ads.

Select **Manual** targeting.

When you choose manual targeting, you unlock more ad options down below. Remember this, because a week from now you might be thinking "Am I going crazy? How do I get those category ads I wanted to try? How do I get the option to write an ad blurb?" It all happens when you hit 'Manual' targeting.

Step 5: Ad format

You can choose **Custom text ad** or **Standard ad**. A standard ad has no supporting text, or 'ad copy' or 'ad blurb'. I like to write short ad copy. It may not be relevant for you to do this, especially if your cover explains exactly what your book is about. For instance, a non-fiction book called HOW TO MAKE AMAZON ADS shouldn't need much more explaining. Fiction books and children's books tend to benefit from ad copy in my experience.

Be aware, however, *your ad copy won't always be shown.*

Click **custom text** to get the option to write ad copy. You could select one sentence from your book blurb, or customize (flash fiction) your book blurb. If you want a smooth transition from click to buy, *your ad copy should agree with what your book blurb proposes.*

Step 6: Choose the book you want to advertise

Books you select from your bookshelf page will show up by default but if you opt out of ad copy you can have more than one product receive the same advertising treatment. This essentially creates a bunch of replica ads with a non-compete clause on them but, as I mentioned, no ad copy.

If you use ad copy you can only pick one product, but perhaps you've changed your mind and want to swap in another book or the paperback version. I suggest you select your bestselling book in its bestselling format. We often don't really know why one book performs better than another, but let's work on boosting your bestselling book first. Logically, if you have a series, you'll pick the first book in your series.

Lastly, if you don't see your book in the list to choose from, just search. It's a glitch.

Step 7: Bidding

The first thing you want to do here is put your default keyword bid way down. If you take nothing else from this book please take this: the default bid is always crazy high. When I first wrote this book I noted the default had increased, the last update I noted it was at 75 cents and when I made the clip below it is at $1.33. This is way too high. Toggle to **Custom bid** as you see in grey box below and in this example I'm going to change the default bid to 18 cents.

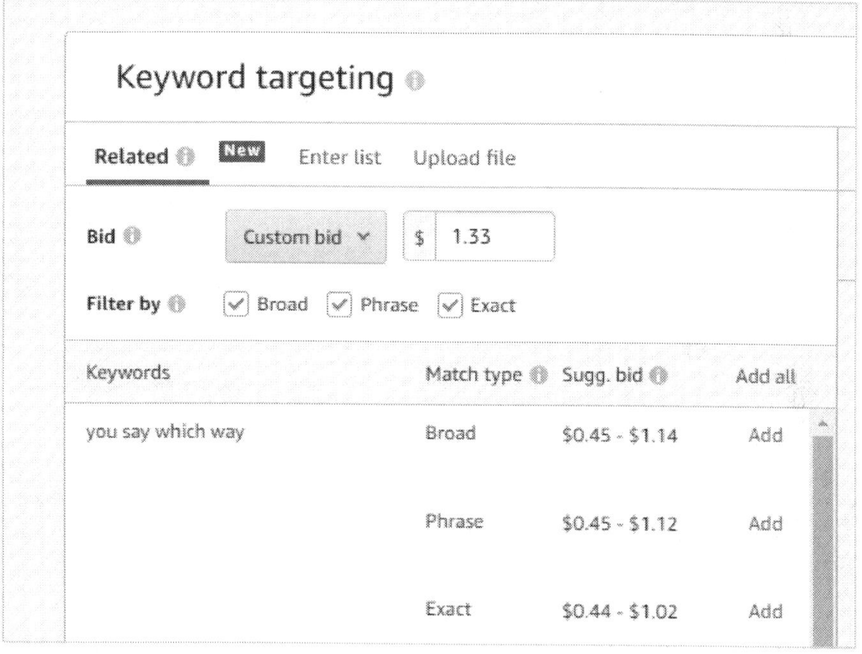

Here is the ad in progress (below) with default bid turned down, and I've also disabled Phrase and Exact. I'm keeping it simple. Not just for you! I often only use Broad alone. You can add Phrase and Exact later.

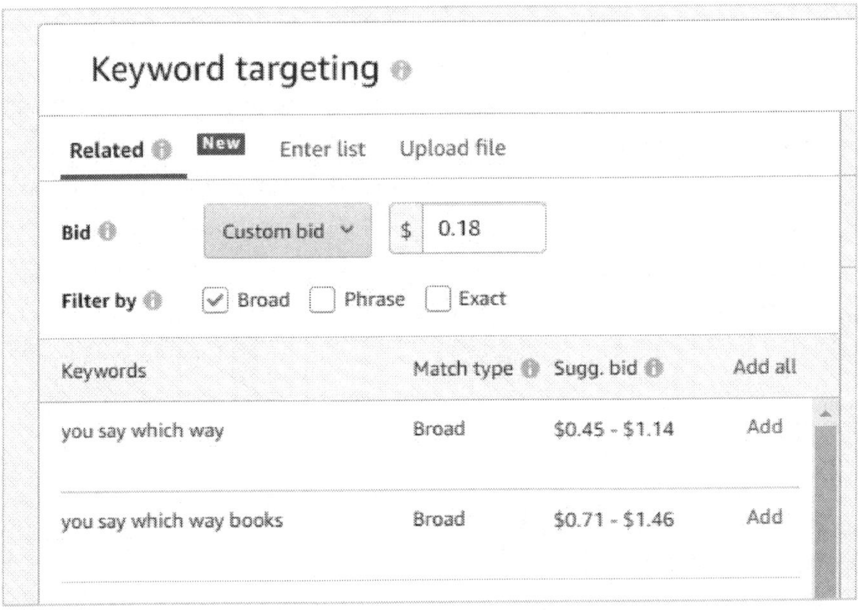

I have never paid more than about 30 cents on a bid (on purpose). The lowest you can set a bid to is 2 cents. Go ahead and choose a low 10 cent bid. Unfortunately, these days you aren't likely to get any impressions for 2 cents.. Don't worry about getting this right though—later when your ad is live you'll be able to adjust your bids. Let's just put in a low default bid and move on. If you are in a popular genre, the cost of a click for popular and obvious keywords will be high.

Above the default keyword bid you'll see a box you can tick for Campaign bidding strategy. Amazon will increase your default bid to get more impressions if you enable it.

Don't. Wait till you have a lot more market information.

Step 8: Keyword targeting or product targeting

Let's go with keyword targeting for starters and come back to product targeting.

Step 9: Adding keywords

Wooooohoo! You made it. I'll just give you the basics here and add a longer discussion later.

You are looking at three tabs. The first is a list of suggestions from Amazon—even though you said you didn't want an **auto ad**. It's worth checking out this ever-evolving list of suggestions. More on that later too. Let's click on the middle tab, **Enter keywords**:

Click on the Enter keywords tab and add some words.

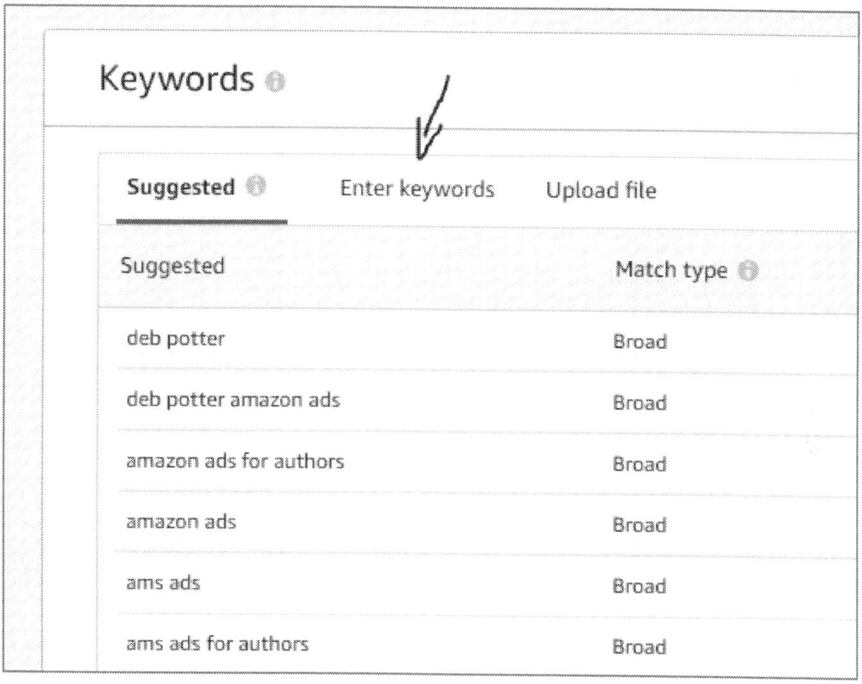

Keywords

Suggested | Enter keywords | Upload file

Suggested	Match type
deb potter	Broad
deb potter amazon ads	Broad
amazon ads for authors	Broad
amazon ads	Broad
ams ads	Broad
ams ads for authors	Broad

A couple of months later, go back and look at the Suggestions again. Chances are that Amazon will give you a slightly better list of suggestions this time. That's because it will gather intel from your own ads. I think you can guess which book I picked to make the screen shot above. I started an ad for this book when I published last year and the list of suggestions is now very sensible. I'm not currently using the second suggestion so I may add it to the ad I already have running for this book.

At this stage, just add 10–20 broad keywords. We just want to get an ad up and running so we can edit it later and learn a bit more about active ads. Some quick ideas could be:

Ideas and themes in your books e.g. quilting, gardening, detectives

- Series names
- Character descriptions (strong women, mother, country girl, scientist, Christian etc.)
- Additional description with your genre e.g. San Francisco thriller
- 'long tail' keywords meaning multiple words, these are often cheaper than single words

Notice that an autocomplete suggestion comes up as you type in keywords. This might give you some great ideas, so slow down and notice what pops up, particularly as a second word. I really like two word combos.

Amazon lets you add up to 1000 keywords, but in places their metadata has gently encouraged less. I would like to firmly suggest you use way less.

You'll see you can toggle to pick between different types of keywords: broad, exact and phrase. Again, there's more coming up on this. I trial keywords as broad generally, but I make an exception and use exact for any authors I want to target. If the book you are advertising has collected a ribbon of 'also bought' books you could add some of those or look for inspiration at the words used in their book blurbs. Try a few variations to describe your genre then STOP! You can add more later, once the ad is running. You don't need to list titles to target in this ad (but you can) because there is a better ad for that. It's called a **product targeting ad**. We'll make one of those next.

Step 10: First edit of keyword bids

When you have a few keywords entered, scroll down again and

you'll see them listed in a new section. Your keywords should have your default bid against them, but to the left you'll now see a suggested bid. If there's no suggested bid, congratulations! You have created an original keyword and Amazon hasn't any suggestions yet. If you keep using the keyword, they'll have data. More likely you haven't been too original and Amazon already has some metrics on your keywords. At this point you can consider Amazon's suggestions. Generally, Amazon will show you a range that the keywords are being bid at, and suggest something mid-range. Set your keywords at the bottom of the range or below the range (depending on how hot your market is). The more original your keywords, and the more of them (long tail) the lower the bid suggestions should be.

Step 11: Negative keywords

This is where you add information about where you *don't* want your ad served. Negative keywords are optional, but you'll want to experiment with them later on.

A negative keyword can help you carve up your category. A writer of sweet romance, for instance, might use hot, erotic, steamy, R18, sexy, etc., as negative keywords. If you write erotica, you might use sweet, clean, friendly, etc. A vegetarian cookbook might use negative keys such as: meat, chicken, bacon, liver, BBQ. Negative keywords are fantastic tools to steer your ads away from showing in the wrong places, and costing you for unwanted clicks.

Step 12: Write your ad

Lastly, you'll enter some ad copy. As time goes by, this is an area you'll obsess on as much as keywords. For now, how comfortable are you about copying the first sentence of your book blurb into the box? If you don't think your book blurb is a useful starting point you may want to revise the blurb soon.

Write a short hook for your book. Read it out loud. Double-check for grammatical correctness and mistakes.

Check your ad blurb against Amazon's rules, which are (in brief):

- No unnecessary capitalization
- No grammar or spelling mistakes
- No claims
- No advertising a cover or product that doesn't meet Amazon standards

Note: the rules about ad acceptability change. Keep up to date on the acceptability policy. If your ad is approved, you won't be able to change your ad copy. That's because Amazon knows some authors would be greatly tempted to put in claims, capitalization, and, in the course of doing this, introduce new grammar and spelling mistakes. Remember, your first ad is just a learning process. We don't expect much from it.

You can take a look at your ad now, in the various ways it might be served, by clicking on **Preview Your Ad.** I find this is a great last-minute check of my ad copy, and I often give new ad text an edit after I've seen how it might deliver.

Did you catch that word 'might' in the last sentence? Your ads are delivered in different ways and your ad text may never be seen. *If you are spending 99 percent of your time crafting blurbs and 1 percent of your time thinking about keywords you have it all backwards.*

Step 13: Launch your campaign

Your ad can take 72 hours to be approved, about 24 hours is the usual wait time, but many ads go through faster. I'd like to think Amazon just trusts me and pops my ads through but it's not just me, lots of my author friends report faster launch of their ads. It isn't automatic though. There's a real person checking it. In February 2019 I had some ads with copy approved in 10 minutes and others in two days. In June 2019 a new ad took one week, in December an auto ad took three days. No idea why. Don't worry, we've got things to do while we wait because we're going to make a better ad.

Just as almost nobody writes a bestseller right out of the gate, your first ads won't be your best. Making good ads uses new word skills and new ways of thinking.

Product targeting (categories and individual products)

Product targeting ads are a more recent addition to Amazon Advertising and may not yet have been well utilized by authors who have been advertising a while. They are a great way to get wide coverage in a category and to target specific books like yours. (Previously keyword ads were used to target other books, but I find product targeting is better suited to this.)

The option to target by category (and individual products) is easy to miss. Here's how to find it and set up an ad:

Choose a sponsored product ad and select the **Manual targeting** option. Next, select **Product targeting**, an option lurking just under 'keyword targeting'. You'll now get what appear to be two more choices to make: categories or individual products. Actually, you can do both in the same ad.

Then pick the tab for **Individual products**, where you can search by author or title and select any book you like. This can save hours of work searching, selecting, and copying authors and titles into regular ads.

Exclude books that are not a good match by adding them as **negative brands**—authors will show up in the list when you type in their names.

Step 1: Campaign name

Make it meaningful. I have CAT in mine as well as a shorthand for the book.

Step 2: Start and end date

There's even less reason for an end date for this type of ad.

Step 3: Daily budget

You'll be able to increase this later, so $10 could be a good starting point, more if your category is very competitive.

Step 4: Targeting

Choose manual targeting for the **product targeting** option to appear below.

Step 5: Ad format

Just like keyword ads, choose whether you want to include ad copy or just have your cover and review stars show up.

Step 6: Choose the book you want to advertise

Be aware that changing your mind about which book you are advertising can change the campaign name to the amazon default name. You can rename it later if this happens.

Step 7: Bidding

Start safely with bid adjustment—down only. That is the default. And, just as we did with keywords ads above, change your default bid to something more conservative. You'll notice that a suggested range will appear once a book is selected. I pick a default under the suggested range and crank up my bids as I learn about the market for each book. In the example below I started at 10 cents. You can see Amazon is tempting me with 39 cents. I selected some categories and many of them showed that a 10 cent bid was within the lower end of the range. I am not taking the bait. In addition, I've enabled Amazon to make an adjustment to the bidding. For top of search I've allowed them a 50% increase for this placement. That means my bid could go as high as 15 cents. My research for this book shows me that it does really well when it shows up top of search. I didn't go for an adjustment for product pages. This is where the majority of my ads will show but I know shoppers often pick their way along and something else shiny could grab their eye after they click on my ad.

Default bid

$ 0.10

Suggested bid: $0.39 Suggested bid range: $0.08 - $1.00

^ Adjust bids by placement (replaces Bid+)

In addition to your bidding strategy, you can increase bids by up to 900%. Learn more

Top of search (first page)	50 %	Example: A $0.10 bid will be $0.15 for this placement.
Product pages	0 %	Example: A $0.10 bid will remain $0.10 for this placement.

Step 8: Keyword Targeting or Product Targeting
Choose product targeting.

Step 9: The next box has two tabs and you can use both in the same ad for different kinds of targeting. First up: categories. You'll probably only get one or two suggested categories in the main box, but you can select a lot more. Only add categories you think have a tight fit with your book. Click **search** to add more categories (with a great fit). Amazon has recently expanded the categories available and it is a FANTASTIC way to target your audience.

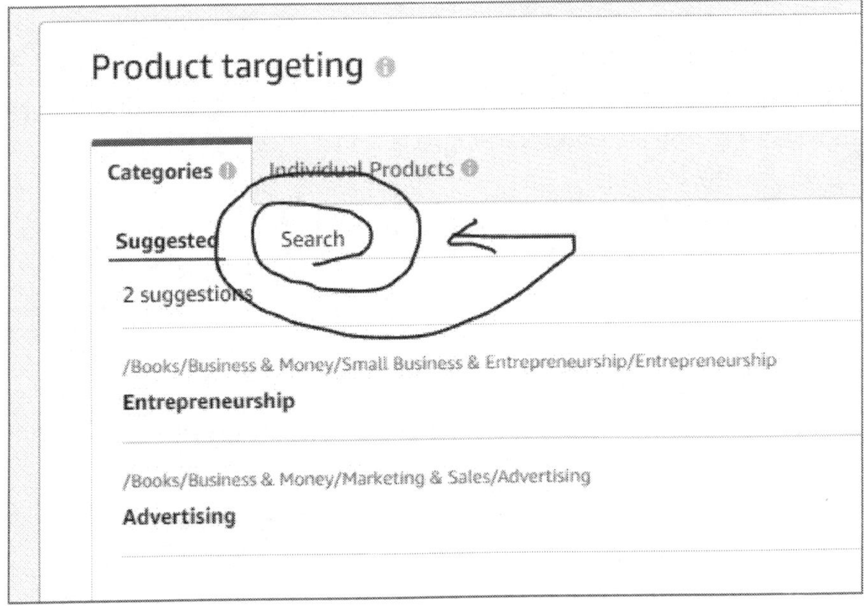

Side note: It can sometimes be hard to know the categories you are in if you requested additional ones and never kept a record. Amazon can give you up to ten, and used to list them all on each book's landing page, but has since stopped. In the days before authors could advertise, authors tended to spread themselves wide. It now pays to be a little tighter to save money on advertising in places you don't fit as well. These ads help you test where you best fit. Meanwhile, back to making the ad:

Choose **individual products** to target by looking at your also-boughts (and the also-boughts of your also-boughts). Amazon suggests this because it has a long history of selling on its platform, so it makes sense to have an 'also-bought' ad. If you make an 'also-bought' ad you might consider ad copy that relates to what you are targeting.

When you've selected everything, you can scroll down to adjust bids (especially important if you forgot to adjust the default bid). Do a final check that your ad name is still showing and then submit your ad.

Note: I like to set these ads to either target books OR hit

categories. That's because I use my daily budgets differently for each. Most of my books are in 'noisy' categories. By that I mean there is a lot of variety in them. I want them to serve a little differently. So even though you can target specific books and get broad coverage in the same ad, I split that functionality out. I also don't like to target too many books or products with one ad. And yes, in some cases I target products. There can be a good fit between non-fiction books and products for instance.

When you get the hang of this type of ad you can add lists of ASINs (the Amazon classification number). There are a few tools you can use for harvesting ASINs, I'll list one I like in the handy tools section.

LOCKSCREEN ADS

Learn from Sponsored Product Ads before you jump to Lockscreen ads. This is important and will save you money.

Lockscreen ads show up on Amazon kindles and their other proprietary reading hardware. The ad appears as the user fires up their device to read, or as little banners at the foot of a screen. They are triggered by the categories of books the owner/s of the amazon account has bought previously. When you set up a lockscreen ad, you pick from a (limited) set of 'interest' categories your ad will target. You give the campaign a lifetime budget and one set bid.

You'll be asked if you want the ad to deliver quickly or gradually. It's a rookie mistake to click the 'quickly' box. Reporting will never be up to date with your spend. If your ad goes rogue you can cancel the ad, but you'll watch your budget continue to drain away and there will be nothing you can do about it. So experiment with lower bids and budgets at first.

Books purchased via an Amazon account can be read on up to eight different reading devices. It's unclear whether Amazon targets the interests of the kindle reader or the account. There may be a mismatch between the interests of a kindle reader and the purchasing history of the account. For instance, if a couple share an account and one likes to read obscure naval war history while the other is a fan of contemporary romance, you wouldn't want to bid against romance to get your naval history book shown. Amazon hasn't given a lot of information about the finer decisions that are made to serve these ads.

If you sell mostly paperbacks, these ads are not going to be useful for you. If you are wide, these ads may not be cost effective. They may not be cost effective if you have only one book—because authors with a first-in-series are prepared to bid high to get read-through to other books.

Lockscreens are currently working better for those happy to run loss-leading campaigns, who already get high-volume sales, and get sales across broad categories. The bidding for Lockscreen ads is highly competitive, by which I mean expensive. My feeling is if they want investment from authors, Amazon have to refine the system. It's relatively new right now, and they will likely make improvements.

Lockscreen ads allow you to write some short ad copy. You could use successful copy you've tried with Sponsored Product ads here (see Blurb Testing in the Strategies section).

I'd like to see the ability to target more precisely before I made more use of Lockscreen ads. Imagine if you could use them to target readers of your own book 2 and 3 with book 4 to make sure readers know it's available? Or those who have chosen to follow your author profile? Amazon is missing my business by not refining these ads.

More about Bidding

You'll see the Bidding section when you set up a sponsored product. The default campaign bidding strategy is set to **Dynamic bids—down only**. That's good, keep it there. **Dynamic bids—down only** is the safest setting to start with.

The default bid is set at 75 cents. That's bad. Turn it down. As you get a better idea of what a good bid might be in your category you will try higher bids. While you are learning, I suggest 5–10 cents for non-fiction books, 10–15 cents for other books, and, for highly competitive markets like romance and thrillers, you will have to go much higher just to get impressions. Not 75 cents, though.

There are authors bidding over $1. These authors generally have huge read through over multiple books and they bid high on book 1. This might be you eventually, but I've helped a lot of authors over the past two years and I've ALWAYS found a way to run low cost ads. Always. The trade off is number of impressions. I don't have a problem with that. When you start out you need to discover what works, otherwise you are chewing through money without learning much. If the day comes that you want to bid over a dollar for a click you'll want to do that with high confidence that you are targeting the right places.

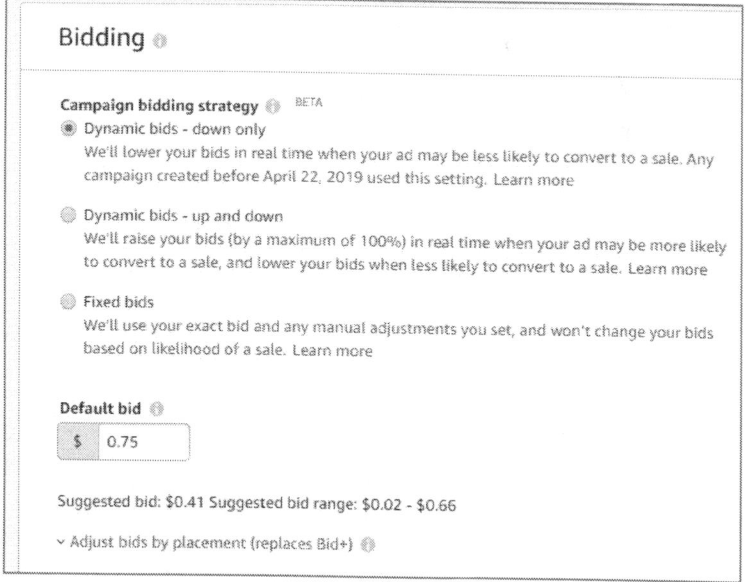

People say that advertising is getting more expensive. I can tell you that I'm paying more now for most of my keywords. I noted what I was bidding on keywords in 2016 and then logged my average bids again in 2017 and 2018. My bid ranges have moved upwards. However, my impressions have increased too. My appetite for risk has gone up because my knowledge about what works is greater. I still start new keywords pretty low and move them up if they don't get impressions.

I wait to get a good amount of impressions before I decide if the keywords are bringing me royalties. So when people say they have to bid more today than they used to, they likely have greater evidence about what works and are willing to pay more. It won't all be due to author inflation. If you are starting out you shouldn't feel like you missed the gold rush. Start with low bids and wait for your evidence base. I don't see the point in handing Amazon a dime when they will take a nickel.

Authors need to stay tuned to their spend. You will want to begin conservatively. Initially take your bestselling book and invest in advertising it. Ideally learn with something that you already know can sell, and focus on giving it more market exposure. Later, when you've seen what works for that book, you can advertise more titles. Your risk will be reduced because you can apply what you learned from advertising your first book on your second, third, and so on.

Setting up hundreds of ads early on is not a good idea because you will want to play with bids and get a feeling for what you can do in your genre. If you just set up a few and pay attention you'll have information you can scale up with.

Everyone's experience is going to be a little different because our books all behave a little differently in the market. I regularly get a post on our ads Facebook page asking about the average bid. Then I ask: what genre are you in? Are you in KU? What's your rank? How many books do you have? Is it a series? All those things would affect the bid.

If you choose low range bid suggestions, your ad will likely show up most of the time on product pages. If you bid really high, you are more likely to show up at the top of searches. As I'll discuss under analysis, you can get information about placement from your advertising analytics pages. With more information over time, you might want to experiment with dynamic bidding for better placement. Stick with the default at first, though.

6. While your first ads are awaiting approval

You'll get two emails from Amazon about new ads. The first will acknowledge that a new ad has been submitted for review. The second will say in the title that your ad has been moderated. This sounds bad but it really means nothing. Your second email should read something like this:

<Thank you for submitting ads under campaign "MeaningfulNameOfAdf5". Following an internal review, below is the status of your ads as per our Book Ads Creative Acceptance Policies. Below ads are eligible to be served on Amazon.>

The key word you are scanning for is **eligible**.

While you wait for your second email, you can start a spreadsheet or scribble pad to brainstorm keywords and books to target. The part of your brain that's usually making up stories is now going to devote idle time to keyword creation. Personally, that's a big part of the fun of Amazon Advertising for me. If you haven't already, you can also start taking a close look at books like yours to advertise next to.

Most successful authors have read a LOT of books in their genre. I typically read and map out at least five books in a row when I'm thinking about writing something new. I look at how the books I like are ranking, I read reviews to see how readers discuss the books. Now take a look at those books again. Note which are in KU and which are wide – if you are wide you might want to avoid books in KU while you are starting out and if you are in KU you might want to target others in KU to match the readership.

Here's an ideal sequence of events to sell your book. Keep this in mind as you read further and as you make and deploy more ads:

1. You make an ad with your readers in mind.
2. The ad shows up in front of the right reader.
3. The cover, or the ad copy, is relevant to what they were looking for.
4. With a CLICK they arrive at your book's landing page.
5. Your book's blurb delivers what your ad copy (or book cover) promised.
6. The price is right.
7. They click the buy box
   … Or NOT …
   but wait … You get a second (weaker) chance.
8. Some time later, Amazon reminds them about the time they mulled over your book, and they buy.
9. If people buy your book, Amazon deploys your ad more often because it is 'relevant'.
10. And all those readers munch down on your back list.

When I run ads, I'm trying to set up this ad-to-buy pathway. I want to help my kind of readers find my kind of books. *My ad helps them recognize the fit.* Covers, ad copy, and ad destinations all work together to create relevance for readers. Relevance is Amazon's word, not mine. Relevance is what Amazon is looking for. Amazon has gazillions of ads running. Sure, it makes money from ads, but Amazon is about selling stuff and delivering a good customer experience. So, ads don't always serve from the highest bid, relevance comes into play. The internet is full of theories about this thing called relevance. I think if you create a well targeted sales path, you're laying the foundation for a relevant ad.

Amazon favors relevance over dollars.

The rest of this book is mostly about making relevant ads. This will take a little while.

7. More about keywords

BROAD

When Amazon first introduced a basic advertising platform for authors, all keywords were broad. Many authors still mostly use broad keywords. Broad means that matching customer searches must contain *all* of your keywords but may also include *other* terms.

For instance, if you use the keyword 'old fashioned mystery' your ad could show up under a search 'old fashioned mystery for teens'. That's great if you are writing a modern-day Nancy Drew, but if you are writing police procedural set in the UK in the 1890's your broad terms might be better as: Victorian murder mystery, Victorian crime, Victorian mystery etc.

Broad matches give you the widest matches possible. It's tempting to use them in a broad way because it's exciting to get a lot of impressions. Broad terms that work for you can be somewhat mysterious. You would rightly think if a broad term does well, then using the same words as an **exact** would do even better—but it doesn't always work out that way. In part this could be because there are extra words being used alongside your broad terms. To understand how a keyword is working you'll want to pull keyword data out of the analytical reports and see what customers actually searched for. That might give you better ideas for 'exact keywords'.

EXACT

Use exact keywords to match to book and series titles and authors. These words tend to land you on book pages rather than at the top of searches, but sometimes you get lucky. As with all bids, there are sweet spots. You might also discover searches that result in good buys in your analytics. Some authors run a combination of exact and broad for all their 'good' keywords. I run my top twenty keywords across all match types in my top ads. I'm basically lazy on the rest.

Remember you don't need to list books as keywords, though, you can use sponsored product ads with individual products.

I harvest customer search terms from my analytical reports and cycle them back into ads as exact keywords.

I am using product targeting more and more but I still do okay with author names and titles, using exact keywords. It may be that I have legacy ads that just work well.

PHRASE

I think of Phrase as a sort of midpoint between broad and exact. Phrase match will match your ad to a search that contains your keywords *in the same order*, as well as a few extra words. So I might use *grandma history* as a phrase and it might match to: *recording grandma history, taking grandma's history*. (Note that most phrase programs allow plurals.)

NEGATIVE KEYWORDS

Negative keywords are words and phrases that Amazon will NOT match your ad to. You use them to steer away from readership you are not relevant to. They cost nothing and are probably the least used keyword tool in the toolbox. But they are fabulous!

A lot of authors say they never use negative keywords. Many worry negative keywords will harm their ads and they will miss impressions that could have gotten them sales.

I was lucky enough to get an Amazon seller account in the UK a couple of years ago and I got looking at search term information. This was before there was any analytical information available from

Amazon Advertising. One look at how some of my keywords were connecting to searches got me very interested in negative keywords. This helped me think about the sort of negatives that would help me filter out impressions to customers who weren't really interested in my sort of book. Advantage ad settings (at that time) did not apply automatic filters, and I saw a lot of adult material showing up as sponsored ads on children's book pages. *I realized my middle grade ads would be showing under adult books,* and so I got motivated to use negative keywords.

Amazon Advertising US does apply some automatic filters; for instance, the reading age metadata informs placement of children's books, but there is still room for refinement. Think about any strong differences between your books and other books in your categories. If you write about vampires and you share a category with unicorn books, and readers don't tend to read about both, consider using negative keywords. (I really don't know if unicorn readers dislike vampire stories.) If you write sweet romance, you might use 'erotica' and 'steamy' as negatives. If you offer weight loss recipes, you might add 'indulgent' or 'dessert' as negative keywords, etc. I have been reading post apoc lately and I like some themes more than others – if I was writing in this genre there are topics I'd be testing to see if they fit or if I should neg them.

On a cautionary note, don't make your negative keyword something so general that your ad doesn't serve. For instance, avoid words like 'book' and 'read'.

You can add negative keywords to automatic ads and you'll find this very handy. An auto ad can be great or dreadful but it wants to be trained by you. It learns from your other ads and metadata and by you telling it what not to do.

HOW MANY KEYWORDS SHOULD I USE?

It's tempting to generate huge keyword lists to use the maximum number allowable. Rookie mistake. This is certainly an approach, but it can be a time-consuming and costly approach. If you are an author who wishes to spend time on writing, you might stick to 50–100 keywords and build up an evidence base of what works best for you by starting small. Bear in mind that many keyword tools generate a lot of variations on the same idea. A large set of keywords will spread your placement thinly across related terms and you might need hundreds of thousands of clicks to determine which work well and which don't—or frankly never make up your mind at all. I like to build my keywords around themes that relate to the ad copy I'm serving up and my book blurb.

Also consider that most keyword tools don't source from actual Amazon searches. They generally source from Google. There are only a few places where Amazon gives up search term information. The first are individualized search term reports from your Amazon advertising reports tab. Another is the autocomplete suggestion in the Amazon search bar, and the last is the pseudo autocomplete when you enter new keywords. This was improved with the new 2019 dashboard; previously the greyed-out autocomplete suggestions only popped up when you made an ad, not when you came back to add more words to a running ad. I used to keep an ad in draft just to tool around to see what popped up as I typed in new phrases, but now, with the improvements, I can head down this keyword-finding rabbit hole any time I like.

There are always exceptions. The exception is the 'discovery ad'. A discovery ad is a strategy where you harvest or dream up a long list of keywords. You set up an ad and let it run and you keep coming back to see if any of the new words seem to be goodies. As you find good words you transfer them into more discrete ads. Another approach would be to gradually reduce the bids of the non-functioning keywords in your stuffed discovery ad and just leave what works. People use this second method believing that there is a chance that a new ad won't 'turn on' and the magic will be lost.

My experience is that few successful keywords or categories or targeted products are actually mysterious. The ones that work generally make good sense. I'm not sure how sophisticated the ad serving at Amazon is, but a new ad usually gets a chance to prove itself. I find I can introduce a proven keyword to an operational ad, or a new ad, and get it serving.

Adding Batches of Keywords

You can add batches of keywords into ads when you make them, or you can add them later on. You can also copy an old ad and it will bring over all your keywords.

While I sometimes copy an ad and bring over the keywords, an annoying feature you should be wary of is that keywords that you've turned off in the original ad will all be turned back on again in the new ad. Partly for this reason, when I switch a keyword off I often turn the bid right down. It may stay alive but not generating impressions or costing much to run. Learn from me. I'm a person who switched off a keyword bidding at 70 cents and only attracting window shoppers, tire kickers and tourists, then copied that ad to grab the keywords for another title, and the 70-cent bid was alive again and costing me money. Don't be like me. *Turn down your bid every time you switch off a keyword to avoid this trap.*

Notice that you can change the default keyword bid—best done from the campaign settings tab of each ad. I like to bid below the suggested bids and crank my bids up later *if necessary*. I know, I'm repeating myself about this but I'm always meeting people started at the middle of the range and got burned fast.

RESEARCHING TARGETS

I love coming up with keywords for myself and other authors. Authors are really good at this because we are creative people. This is the most fun part of advertising. But I find authors don't always have a lot of faith in themselves. They race off to keyword generators and plug in hundreds of keywords that may or may not be very relevant to their book. Don't get me wrong, those tools can be fabulous, but it really helps if you understand your market, and how your ads are served, before you dive in and get overwhelmed.

Amazon's help section suggests using titles that deliver similar stories to yours, and authors who write like you. This advice was published before **product targeting ads** were available. As I write this, I'm still doing experiments to gauge whether I get better results targeting books in sponsored products (keyword ads) vs product targeting. Product targeting is currently delivering much better results, but this may be because other authors aren't using them yet and Amazon is giving them a little more relevance.

If you are a non-fiction writer, it's likely that people won't need two books on the same topic. (You really only need one *How To Train Your Cat* book to find out that cats can't be trained.) So consider *the value your book offers over other books like yours,* and let people know that value via your ad copy and your book blurb. That's my theory anyway, but recently I visited the home of a friend whose house was wallpapered in bookshelves filled with non-fiction books. He told me when he wants to understand something, he buys several books on the subject. Anyway I like to put my book next to an option where I look better.

If you are a fiction writer, it's likely that people WILL need two books on the same topic. People tend to go on reading jags about the same sorts of things and offering similar pleasures. This desire to get the same joy from a book often drives readers searching.

My best keywords are not authors or titles. They are a result of brainstorming how readers might search for a book like mine. What is their reading joy? How would they describe it? There are many ways to consider this. For my non-fiction, I think about problems that my book solves. What is their problem? How would they ask about it? (This also helps me think up ideas for new non-fiction projects.)

I also put a lot of thought into how someone looking for a book as a gift would refine their search. Who would be the ideal recipients for my books?

Authors tend to describe their books with publishing jargon that some readers know well (e.g. 'sweet romance' and 'cozy mystery') but not all readers know these terms and they search in varied ways. I also add other adjectives to genre jargon; 'new cozy mystery', 'British sweet romance', 'like Game of Thrones'. Amazon, I think, is programmed to prefer exact matches, even when your keyword is broad, and especially when keywords are relatively new.

Off-the-beaten-path keywords have served me very well. They don't tend to get a lot of impressions, but the Click Through Rate (CTR) is awesome, suggesting they get served at the top of pages because they are closest to what was searched. They also don't cost much.

A good CTR gives your ad brownie points with Amazon. It's a signal your ad is relevant.

You might consider starting a keyword discovery group. I find this can work best when you aren't in the same genre, because authors in the same genre might be happy to share general tips but they won't be keen to share their best keywords.

My working title for this book was 'unicorn unicorn' because doubling keywords was something I took more than a year to discover for myself. I rang a friend one day, really excited, to suggest she try 'dragon dragon' (guess what she writes about?) and she told me she'd been using it forever. Amazon had suggested 'dragon dragon' in her ad suggestions. Doubling keywords might work because Amazon doesn't actually read them as doubled, just two words that match a search or match with words on other book blurbs. Amazon might see doubled words as more relevant. So: try doubling some of your super relevant words.

An often-talked-about triple keyword combo is 'book book book'. It gets a lot of impressions because the word book shows up multiple times on Amazon book pages. Be warned, though, it's very general (read: meaningless). If you want to be served up willy-nilly and you have money to burn, use 'book book book'. Don't bid much for it, though. I would rather throw my money at category targeting.

Reviews are another place to look for keywords. The positive words readers choose to use when describing your books might be how others would understand them and describe them. If you don't have a lot of reviews, just look at books like yours.

Seasonal keywords are always worth considering. You can deploy these before and during a season: 'great holiday reads', 'light holiday reads', 'summer reading', beach reading' and also *after* a season 'more like Game of Thrones', 'more like Big Bang', etc.

Once you have run a few ads, you can look at your advertising reports to see what readers searched by—more on this below under analysis.

Your keyword list is something that you'll grow over time. It's very possible to come up with a bunch of words that will give a well edited, proofed story, with a professional cover, a moderate increase in sales and downloads. You don't need to discover them all at once. The discovery process is fun. I'm still walking down the street and a new keyword idea pops into my head. I speed up. I can't wait to get home and throw it into an ad.

I'll cover more about how to use different sorts of keywords in the strategy section.

8. Analysis

I know some people shrink away from math, but our inner Archimedes comes out when it's all about MONEY. Simple analysis can get you far with Amazon ads. I use Excel, so that's what I'll talk about here. Other spreadsheet products out there will all be able to do the basic stuff I describe too. And it is basic! You can do a lot by sorting columns of information different ways.

Human beings aren't natural statisticians. We tend to go by hunch and anecdata. It helps to set up tests, and to test the things you feel you are seeing. While a lot of author friends say they aren't analytical, I think they often are but don't realize it. Successful authors know how to write to market, which means they follow rules about audience expectations. They learn the rules by recognizing patterns. That's analysis. That is all it is.

Authors often plan word counts for the day, run project plans to produce multiple books per year, do taxes and work with budgets. So don't tell me you don't have a math brain. I think it's just that people don't know their way around Excel and expect something is coming that will stump them. What I outline below won't stump you.

THE BASICS

If you don't already, start keeping your own sales records. It's useful to keep monthly sales of paperbacks, eBooks and page-read counts (if in Unlimited) for *each title* and by *each market* (e.g. each country). Maybe you've always been meaning to start doing this. Don't hesitate, make a start. If you've been selling awhile, get your sales data from Amazon and put it in an excel spreadsheet.

Since I first published this book I hear people say oh you're so lucky you've kept records, that would be a huge enormous job for me to go back and make the records, I need to spend my time writing.

Well, I didn't keep records the first few years but when I started getting regular checks and had a few more books planned I made a start and at the end of every month I'd record my sales and then I'd go back and add in the history of just one month. In that way it wasn't an arduous task and I had the satisfaction of seeing the pattern of two more months at a time.

Splitting your sales records by country is important because they all have different sales patterns. My best seller in Germany is a book that doesn't sell much at all in the US and is middling in the UK.

Numbers are great, but authors know words help too. Every month I write myself a diary entry about how my publishing business, the Fairytale Factory, has performed and what I've been up to. I say if I've sold more books than that month the year before. I note any promotional work I've done which might explain things. I note books that are being worked on and where they are at. I note things that have gone on that might have affected sales. I even write down ideas I haven't acted on because writing things down makes me evaluate my ideas, and it often leads me to the first step I need to take. The point is my brain isn't going to remember that Netflix ran an amazing show called Bandersnatch that caused interest in my book about writing interactive fiction. If I don't sell so many copies of that title a year from Bandersnatch, I'll have a way to know it's because there wasn't an unexpected external event boosting sales. This process gives me context when I look back and it gives me a time once a month to reflect and think about goals for the next four weeks.

When I started advertising with Amazon, I had already been keeping sales records, so I knew my annual patterns really well. If you don't know much about sales for your genres, I suggest you have a google and ask other authors. NY Times bestseller data and household economic surveys tell us that books generally enjoy peaks around Christmas and other gift-giving holidays, and that sales are better in winter than summer. Some genres are less likely to be bought as gifts (think erotica and romance) so these books can actually taper off during Christmas as people channel their spending toward others. I have seen reading taper off during the Olympics, some parts of the election cycle of different countries, and I've seen them go up when there are big weather events keeping people indoors. I often see sales pick up before a holiday and slump during the break when people are no longer buying—they are reading. My worst sales day two years running? New Year's Day. Second worst? Good Friday. (Christmas day is good. People have new reading devices with which to download eBooks, and others still seem to be Christmas shopping.)

Now that you're advertising, another very handy metric to keep on hand is the amount you earn, from each Amazon store each month, tax that was prepaid on your behalf, and the amount you spent on advertising each month. This gives you a high-level picture of whether you are winning or losing. Don't wait till tax time to figure this out, it's useful now. There is some lag in recording this stuff so you can also look at month to date profits (estimating page reads) vs ad spend on the advertising dashboard.

I also keep a record of what each book cost me to publish. The book needs to recover that expense before it starts making a profit. If your cover and editing cost you $1000, advertising has cost you $200 and you get a check for $1200 you haven't made a profit, you've only recouped your costs.

You'll come across the phrase 'statistically significant results' being banded around among Amazon ad users. This can sound very complicated. They only mean that they *have observed a pattern over time with a great deal of impressions and clicks.* That's all.

Amazon can do a lot of analysis because they know a lot more than us. Amazon knows how its system is set up, how many are bidding and how high, what sales are like in a category overall. We don't know all that stuff. But human beings are pretty good at spotting patterns over time. If we stop and think about it with our practical hat on, we can hazard pretty good guesses between correlation and causation.

If you change your bids around a lot you will not have as good a pattern over time from which to draw conclusions.

Something you can do to make your observations a little more consistent is ensure you create the environment to observe a pattern over time.

One way to do this is by keeping some of your ads static, not playing around with bids and introducing new words and pausing others. In the beginning this is a good tactic as you build up your knowledge. If you bid low and set a high daily budget in your first ads, and ONLY change the budget and not the bids early on, you'll start to develop an observable pattern.

Ideally, I'd like to tell you to freeze everything for the first month but I have seen an observable pattern with everyone I've coached and it goes like this: they start off cautious with a low daily budget like $5 a day and small bids or 2 and 5 cents. A week later with no impressions they are frustrated and want to make changes, crank up the bids and the budget.

Rampant changes ensue. Another week goes by and the first sale happens and they are scratching their heads trying to work out how to replicate that sale.

When an ad is up and running, the click data can lag a little (there is hot debate on this) and the sales can be attributed up to 14 days later. If a reader clicks an ad and buys any of your books within 2 weeks it will be attributed to the ad. So while you might know you made a change to the budget two weeks in, and cranked up the keyword bids, and the sale came two days after that, *you do not know if your sale occurred during the first environment you set up or the changes you made later.* So while I do make changes to my bids quite frequently, I also leave them alone long enough to make some observations. I will change something that looks like its running away without making money but I don't micro tweak on a daily basis.

Customizing and Reading the Campaigns Tab

The Campaigns tab is very customizable and where you'll spend a lot of time. From here you can create new campaigns, look at the performance of all your ads at once, and dig into the detail of running ads.

Date range

One customizable aspect you'll use a lot is the date range. Heads up: if your dash ever seems to freeze or not update, toggle the date range a bit. It's an occasional quirk I hear people report. When you start ads, I suggest you set the date range to lifetime for a while. Once you get the hang of it, you'll spend a lot more time using 'this month' and 'last thirty days'.

I like to monitor my individual ads over 30 days if they are getting good traffic, and I also look at longer periods to get the observable patterns.

Use the shortest available time period to check that an ad is still getting regular impressions. Set to 7 days and ask: Are you alive? Yes, I am!

The 'lifetime' time period is great for looking at keywords over time because there will be a lot more impressions. It's tempting to make decisions on only a few clicks—especially clicks without buys. Really, you want to stay with a keyword through good times and bad—*especially if it makes intuitive sense to you.* (Hint: If the keyword is 'book book book' it makes no sense.)

Monthly, I take a look at impressions for my author name, and the other authors I write with, our titles and brands. From this, I get a little bit of an idea of the traffic hitting my page.

It took me a while before I understood the value of using my own pen names and titles as keywords. If a reader has managed to get to your page, you don't want them distracted away from it by ads asset by different author. You paid for the click that got them to your page—

either through an ad or your writing. You want them to buy one of your books. An Amazon advertising guy told me that people often search for another book by searching an author or a title they enjoyed. That makes sense to me. If they search your name or the title of the last book they read by you, you want to show them the next book you have on offer.

Customizing the charts and metrics

Change the metrics displayed in the main graph by clicking on them. To get more options, drop a metric out by clicking the x in the top right corner—you'll then get to add a new metric option. Warning: graphs that show two different stories look slick but are very often misleading.

The two metrics might not relate well to each other and, even if they are about related concepts, the scales are different. This is the case with Amazon charts. However your brain will often try and pull some sense out of double axis charts. Also, I find the graphs much more useful when looking at individual ads. For instance all the information below is interesting to me but graphing the two highlighted items doesn't tell me much.

The date range of the main chart can be changed when you play with the options underneath it (see the snip below). Clicking **columns** changes the data displayed for individual campaigns directly below the main graph. It can take people a while to discover this and when you do you'll become more discerning about which metrics are most useful to you.

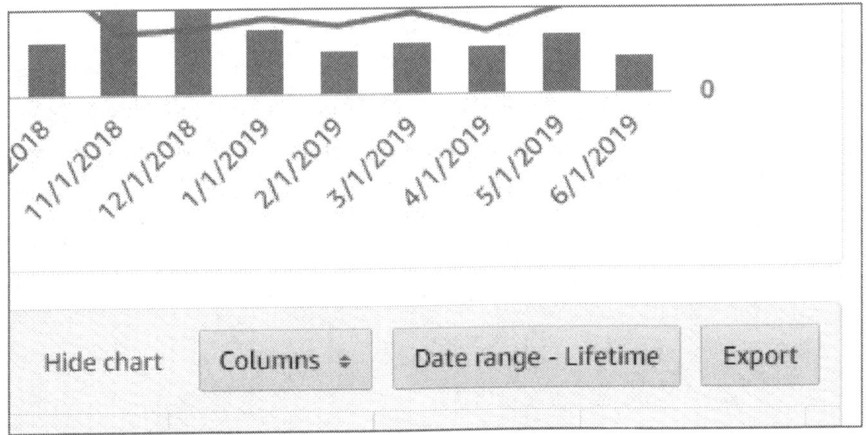

Search bar

The little campaign search bar can be used to search for specific campaigns *as long as you have good shorthand for your campaign names.* When you have a lot of ads this is very handy. If you are muttering to yourself "yeah I wish I could turn back time," and you have a collection of badly named ads there is hope! You can rename your ads on the **Campaign Settings** tab.

Individual campaigns

Although it's fun to see how many impressions and clicks you've gained over time, the high-level dash is too high-level to make good decisions with if you are advertising more than one book.

Under the main graph, you can customize what you see in the ads list. The columns button lets you select different metrics like CTR, ACOS, impressions, CPC, etc. This information is well worth building an understanding about and monitoring.

Once you click on a keyword ad, you can take a look at the **targeting** tab and see what your keywords are up to. You can add more keywords and you can adjust individual bids. You can reset the default bid for keywords under the **Campaign Settings** tab. It is absolutely worth setting this. This stuff just takes a bit of patience to get used to. Make some more test ads and see what happens. Keep your bids low at first and likewise your daily budget.

The **Campaign Settings** tab also allows you to view your ad—very handy if you didn't give your ad a meaningful name and you wonder what your ad copy says, and, you can rename your ad on this tab. Even if you gave your ads great names to begin with, you might want to put high level clues in an ad's name later when you switch it off for a while or it houses a test you've made.

Suggested bid

Status	Suggested bid	Bid	Impressions
			137,954
Delivering	$0.59 $0.44-$0.81 Apply	$ 0.30	1,124

If you enable the suggested bid column you'll see ranges for keywords and a midpoint you could apply with one click. As you can see in the **example I'm getting impressions from a bid well under the range.** This ad was set to 30 days when I made the snip. I got more than 1000 impressions for that keyword at nearly 30 cents less than Amazon suggested.

Occasionally, if I'm getting good results from a keyword but Amazon suggests a much higher bid, I will jack it up for a couple of days to get more impressions. Then I drop the bid down again. I'm baiting for relevance. I don't want to pay 44 cents for this keyword. I just want to teach Amazon that the keyword has relevance. It's easy to forget you've done something like this. I set a meeting alarm on my cell phone to remind me to bring the bid back down.

Below are my standard column settings for reviewing individual ads over their lifetime. You can also see that one keyword combo accounts for about one third of the orders/sales for this book. I have 128 live keywords for this ad but about 7 are doing all the work. The keyword with the 12 percent click through rate is for my own brand name. Loving that 1 percent ACOS too!

I like to look at my ads over their lifetime to help me make decisions about whether products or keywords or categories convert into clicks and sales. If you are mostly getting royalties from page reads you'll want to look at the clicks but if you also sell books, you have the hard proof of orders.

Each of these lines can tell you a story and give you market insights. My author name didn't deliver so many impressions but the CTR is so high it pretty much ensures Amazon will keep delivering it to me at 11 cents.

Hide chart | Columns | Date range - Lifetime | Expo

Impressions	Clicks	CTR	Spend	CPC	Orders	ACOS
1,786,872	6,132	0.34%	$1,206.51	$0.20	936	8.48%
308,828	1,983	0.64%	$441.60	$0.22	286	10.39%
63,077	438	0.69%	$101.61	$0.23	108	6.31%
57,151	415	0.73%	$87.90	$0.21	96	5.82%
47,332	300	0.63%	$67.88	$0.23	64	7.09%
438,575	571	0.13%	$66.41	$0.12	58	7.66%
702	85	12.11%	$9.34	$0.11	50	1.01%
102,082	360	0.35%	$71.02	$0.20	43	11.05%

KEEPING KEYWORD LISTS

As you find effective keywords, you might like to keep a list of them. I use Excel. I have to admit I've been kind of lax. I just make a note of the keywords I discover that are AWESOME rather than a list of every keyword I've ever used. I think there are likely keywords that

I've used and not seen their potential for awesomeness because I haven't bid enough and/or I've tested at the wrong time of year, so I just didn't get enough impressions to notice them. *I am not too worried about the ones that got away.* I work on optimizing the words that work, and try to get them running as efficiently as possible. I might have taken a different approach if I'd planned from the start and if I had brainstormed using Excel. Instead I have tended to brainstorm with a new ad open in front of me and a shiny new ad blurb. You could be a lot more strategic. If I get a chance to use a time machine, I will send my 2015 self a copy of this book. Hmm, a time machine postal service, that's a good story idea.

So my lists are retrospective, tight and manageable. I have different lists because I have books in different genres, and both fiction and non-fiction.

I use the lists if I want to upload a new ad. I also look at the list and think about why something works. Can I do more with that? Is there another way to get that result? Can I be more specific?

THE ADVERTISING REPORTS TAB

Advertising reports shine great big searchlights on how your ads are working. They are so exciting! You can see which of your keywords triggered your ad to be served against customer searches. When that happens, you get data on what customers search for. If you watch your ad reports, that sets up a virtuous cycle to improve your campaign performance.

Go to the **Advertising reports** tab of the Amazon Advertising dash. Click on the three little lines on the top left:

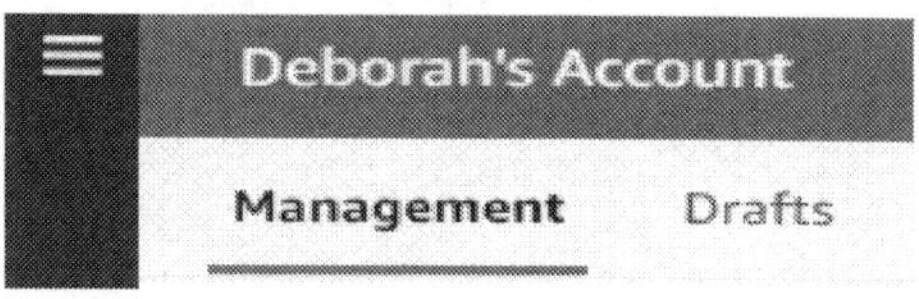

and then reports:

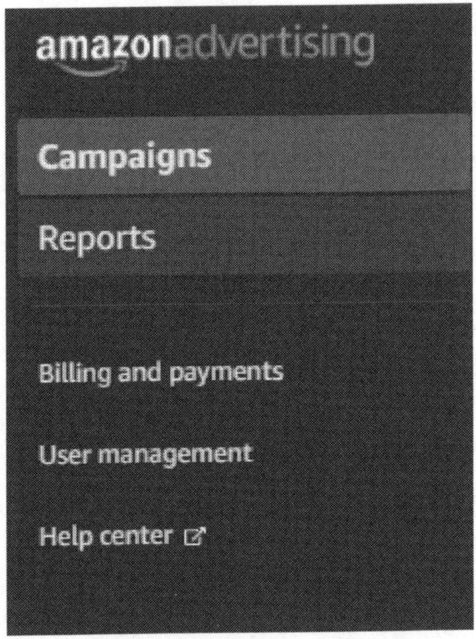

Start with the default **search term** report and 'all sponsored product campaigns' (you can easily sort later, it's too time-consuming now). Set the dates for as long as the report will let you (usually only a couple of months) because we want to *observe a pattern over time.* Hit 'create report' and watch the data being retrieved. A report will now appear below and stay available forever (or quite a long time). Open the report and save it.

The first time you look at these reports is like that moment just after Ali Baba said Open Sesame! He steps into a cave of treasure. Here's how to find your treasure.

With the report open, run your cursor over the top line so you have all the column headings highlighted. On the home tab ribbon of Excel go to the very right and select the AZ Filter option. Just hit Sort & Filter, and then the Filter icon. Ta da! Every column heading now has a filter on it.

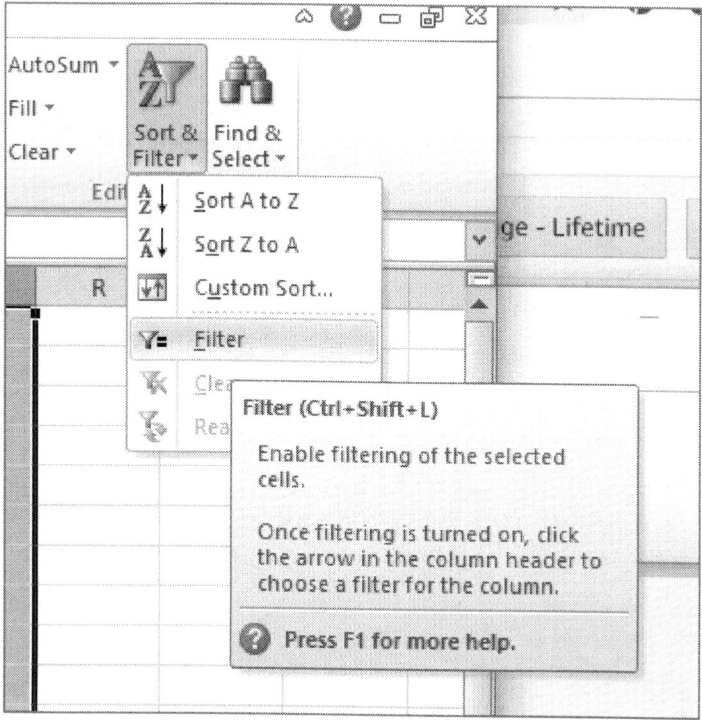

Your sheet should look like the following example. I've circled some active filters (first wobbly circle) and the currently active sort (second wobbly circle). As long as you have filters across all of the active columns of your table, you can sort without scrambling any rows.

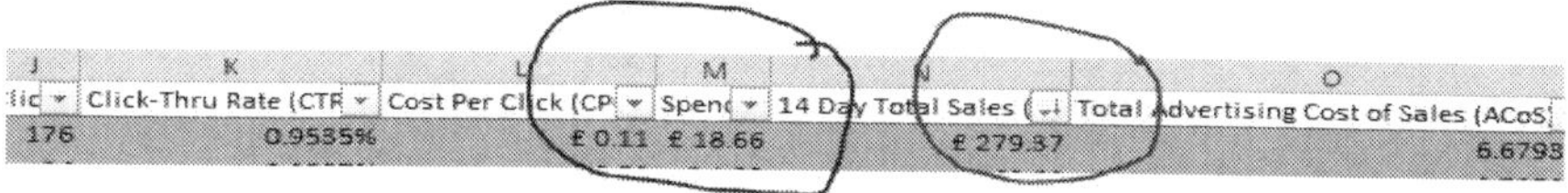

At this point, I often highlight columns I don't care much about and hide them. For instance, columns A-D aren't very useful (to me) so I hide them by highlighting the letters above each column heading, right clicking, and selecting hide. This creates a more manageable set of columns. Don't worry, all the hidden columns are acting like the ones you can see, it's not scrambled eggs under there.

Then use COLOR and SORTING to find things out.

Head to column Q. If your Excel sheet looks like mine, the heading should be TOTAL ORDERS. Sort that column highest to lowest. Ping! The spreadsheet takes all the info across all the rows and prioritizes by orders (BUYS). Those are interesting. If you've done this right, over on column O, the ACOS column, only those rows that made sales have an ACOS. Let's give all that info a color. Highlight the rows (just highlight the numbers of each row) and change the color to green by selecting the little paint pot icon on the top ribbon. The info in the green rows made sales. (Note: this is not telling you about what gave you page reads but it makes sense that those terms that make sales also make page reads, so this column still gives you good clues.)

So now go to column H: CUSTOMER SEARCH TERM and read all those green customer search terms. Do they make sense to you? Do those terms have something to do with your books? I hope so! If they do, copy those terms into a new spreadsheet entitled 'what worked'. Then put them into new ads.

You'll also see how many impressions you got with the terms. It isn't giving you any indication of how often the term was searched, just the impressions you got for the term. If you bid more for those terms, it's possible you'll get more impressions. Use your common sense and consider how rare the term might be. Most of those terms won't seem unlikely. Depending on how sure you are that they are a good fit, you might consider a higher bid. Start low, and gather an observable pattern over time.

Column K is interesting too, especially for those getting page reads. It shows the CLICK THROUGH RATE. If it's close to 100 percent it's great. I have a few like that, but I have plenty that are very low, under 1 percent! Quite possibly a lot of ads are served and the readers never even saw them. When the click through rate is high and the keyword has high relevance to your books, there's more reason to consider a higher bid. If you mainly get page reads rather than buys, you will want to look at CLICK THROUGH RATE more than TOTAL ORDERS.

Okay, time to mix it up. Regardless of sales, which terms got you the most clicks? Have a look at the table and figure that out.

Column J tells you which terms got you the most clicks. If you're like me, you might end up deploying the same keywords over multiple ads. So you might need to add a few together.

(If you ever see that rows contain a mix of green and white, you'll know they got scrambled somehow, but while you see stripes, you'll know everything is good. I find people new to Excel have trouble believing its awesome sorting skills.)

If you are in KDP Select, high CTR items might have given you page reads. Just think if they are relevant, do those terms make sense to you? Also, think to yourself if they are NOT relevant. If there seems to be some confusion and mismatch, you could consider making the search term a negative keyword. Don't be too hasty, though. Ask yourself if you are seeing an observable pattern over time.

Lastly, look at your spend. Does it seem intuitive that the keywords that are costing you money are a good fit with your book? As an example, I use the very broad term 'chapter book' in some of my ads for middle grade interactive fiction books. While the stories are constructed of tight sections between choices, they are not strictly chapters. Some people would definitely not think they were chapter books. I have found that I get a lot of clicks (high CTR) but the conversions to orders aren't high. The evidence for 'chapter books' is murky. I still use it, but I don't bid very high. This is a term I use inside a high budget and low bid strategy ad (see Strategies).

If you mostly get royalties from page reads and you have a high CTR for something but no buys you should be very sure there's a really tight fit with your book. You can run experiments by switching off terms that don't have a few sales and seeing if your page reads drop. When I do this I alternate by month for a few months to check. The lower the volume of page reads you get the longer you need to experiment.

If you download and look at customer search term information over time (I do it at the end of the month), then you'll gather information about search terms that work for you by accumulating the evidence to say yes! I see a regular observable pattern.

Downloading customer search terms is extremely useful to do in times of high sales activity. I reckon the servers at Amazon HQ are practically glowing over winter and the Christmas sales period.

I avidly read all customer search terms. I read everything in the column. This column tells me about the behavior of real people who use Amazon to find and buy books. I often get ideas for new keywords from column H (CUSTOMER SEARCH TERMS). Several times I've found products (brands of books) with high conversion rates that I've gone on to target.

If you are not in KDP Select or you don't get too many page reads (for instance you sell a lot of paperback coloring books or children's books) then there is a whole lot less intuition required to read the Search Term reports.

Keep in mind that an order can be for any of your books—not just the advertised book. This also explains why one click could generate sales for more than one book. It could be anything on your KDP account the customer bought over the 14-day period by the same pen name.

Another report type you can generate is for keyword analysis. Follow the steps above and swap in 'targeting' instead of 'search terms' and then download a different analysis report. Add filters to the table you generate in the same way, looking at what definitely made you sales, CTR and where you spend money. This information shouldn't be surprising. You can see it playing around in each individual ad on the Campaigns tab. It is good seeing the info collated.

Previously, if you wanted to have some sense of the effect of changing your keyword bids, you needed to start new ads with the new bids.

Now, if you are disciplined, you could tweak your keyword bids once a month and then generate reports to see how they are doing.

Optimization has been one of my most successful strategies, and I'm just starting to use this report to do it in a more disciplined way.

Another report I find very insightful is the **placement report**. The first time I pulled up one of these gave me a major 'ah ha' moment. The report tells you, for all your ads, where your ad has been showing up. In my case most of my ads are landing on product pages and a small percentage in search lists. Search lists show the most buys, though.

While 80 percent of my Sponsored Product ad placement occurred on a product page in January 2019, *that last 20 percent accounted for 71 percent of my sales.* If this turns out to be your pattern too, you might want to bid higher by placement. An ad with a tight curated set of products or keywords is the best candidate for this kind of bidding strategy.

You don't always want to pay to be placed in a search. If someone wants a Margaret Atwood book, they don't want my time travel offering. They want Margaret. A lower bid to show up on her product pages might be more productive.

If all this seems like too much hard work perhaps I can tempt you with smaller snippets of data. If you click all the way in to a running campaign on your ads page you'll see two options on the left, Search terms and History.

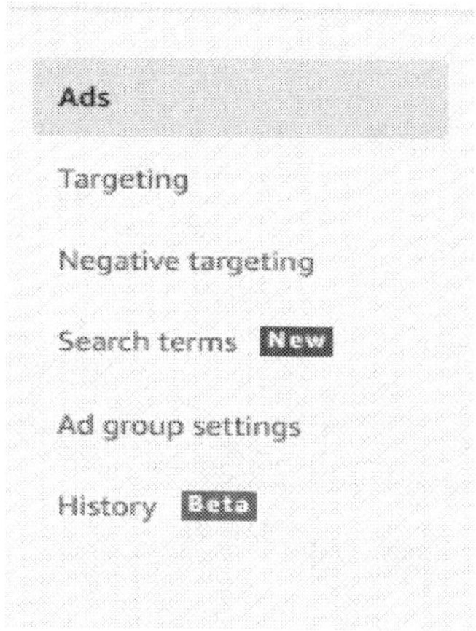

Search terms gives you info about that ad's recent fraternization with targets and keywords. You can even export the info right there. I personally like taking a look once a month, but while you are building knowledge this might give you some quick insights. Since these insights might get you changing your bids or adding new targets, the History offering can be useful too. You can check your History to see if you lowered a bid like you were thinking you might or raised it already. People forget stuff. The history window is only about 30 days but I have found it useful at busy times such as when I'm testing a new book.

IS YOUR AD IN THE RED OR THE BLACK?

When you've got some functioning ads, you need to know whether they are making you money or costing you money. In this section I'll focus on understanding the actual cost of your ad without considering any boost to sales you might get (such as read through to other books in your series, and sales from increased visibility). It's really important you are able to gauge how far your ads are eating into your royalties, or worse, costing you money. From some of the crazy high suggested bids I see, I suspect a lot of people don't figure this out early on.

Amazon reps have this phrase you'll hear often: 'It depends on your goals for your campaign'. Even if your goal is to get as visible as you can and lose money trying, I'm sure you'd like to be able to tell your accountant how much you lost. My goal is to run ads that get my books in front of readers who like stuff like mine, and get enough sales not only to cover the cost of the ads, but to make me money.

Let's start with ACOS. ACOS is the percent of sales spent on advertising. *It is not the portion of your royalty spent on advertising.* There is no royalty data in the advertising dashboard, that's over in the KDP dash and the two don't join up. We have to do that. We join it up.

If you mostly earn money from page reads, ACOS is not going to tell you a jot, but stay with me. The concepts here are useful.

Establishing ACOS threshold guides

If you make the majority of your income from paperbacks or eBook sales (as opposed to page reads), ACOS is very useful, but you need to work out what a good ACOS is. Each of my paperbacks makes a slightly different royalty because of their varied production costs (length, format, etc). Every book, therefore, has a different 'break even' ACOS.

Simple example

For instance, Amazon sells one of my paperback books for $9.05. Let's call it BOOK A. The royalty for BOOK A is $3.28. Amazon clips off another 5 percent in my case for the American tax system. This means I'm going to see about $3.12 in royalties, which is about 34 percent of the sale price. When I look at ACOS I will have that 34 percent in my mind.

ACOS is the percentage of attributed sales (not royalties) that was spent on advertising. If my ad for the $9.05 BOOK A has an ACOS of about 30 percent I'm about breaking even on the ad. If the ACOS is over 34 percent *it is costing me money to run.* If it's under 30 percent, I'm making money from my ads for BOOK A. Ideally my ACOS for the paperback is well below 30 percent.

If I normally sell a certain book every day with no advertising, and advertising improves that to two books a day, then the ACOS threshold I calculated above is something I should pay a lot of attention to. If I start selling a lot more of BOOK A as a result of advertising (I assume), then I might accept an ACOS nearer to break even.

A little more complicated example

Another book I have, BOOK B, sells about 90 percent paperback but also sells quite a few eBooks and gets revenue from page reads. I make more from an eBook than a paperback with this book. About double. But I sell more paperbacks. I can't tell from the ad report whether I've sold an eBook or a paperback through the ad. I have no information about page reads. I also don't know if the sales are read through to other books in the series. Amazon has not made this easy. Yet.

But you can still make yourself some rules to follow.

Being conservative, I assign the lowest ACOS (from the paperback sales) and use that as a maximum threshold to work with advertising BOOK B. This is an example of setting a threshold guide for a book without all the information I have to establish a guide like the example above for BOOK A.

Next to my laptop I've got a list of books and their percentage profit after tax. Your sales profile won't be like mine. You might sell more eBooks. You might make more money from page reads.

If you have a five book series and you make $2 on each, and a read through rate of 50% you might say you'd spend up to $4 on a click. Some people spend this, and more. Genres where the top 100 are dominated by authors with a big back catalogue and plenty of series can be hard to break into for this reason. (See Staircasing in the tips section along with info on advertising a series.)

Establishing thresholds using retrospective data

Your sales history can help if page reads are a significant part of your income. Amazon has made improvements lately, but page read earners still need to do a lot of guesstimation. Even if we had unit download information, we still can't predict how many pages someone might read before they go to another book. I took a few books out of KDP in 2018 and went wide. I still had page reads recorded for those books for months. When someone buys a book, we don't know if they ever read it, but with page reads it's delightful to see those numbers go up and know your words are being read. For analysis though, it is freaking frustrating ('scuse my freak).

If you have a sales history you can estimate the activity you would have had without ads, and the impact of advertising, because ads tend to *amplify the trends* authors experience without advertising. Your best seller is probably going to stay your best seller. That book *you* think is your best but doesn't sell as well as your mediocre book is likely not to change where it ranks in your personal best selling list.

You can use the KDP royalty estimator to bring up estimated royalties to date, to compare to spending to date on ads. I find this is most useful at the beginning of the month when I can look at the *previous* month and then again about halfway through the current month. You adjust your ad to the same time period as the royalty estimator and ask yourself: am I making money or losing money?

I also like to look at KDP reports 'prior months royalties' and estimate the page reads. After a few years working with page reads and foreign currency, I find I can pretty accurately guess what page reads will convert to in US dollars and UK pounds and I'm pretty good at converting these totals to New Zealand dollars. As I said at the start, the inner Archimedes tends to do well when the math problem involves money.

Using the KDP royalty estimator

The KDP royalty estimator beta is a real-time gauge you can use to understand the effectiveness of your ads—deselect all your other books and non-US markets and match your time period with the time period of your advertising dashboard to see what your estimated profit is *minus the cost of your advertising.*

For beginners, this might be one of the easiest ways to see if your ads are in the red or the black. You do still need to go and inspect individual ads activities though.

My big peeve is that the windows you can do this over are restricted to the current month and last month (until royalties have been announced). I get that we get different rates each month but as an estimator tool a 'past 30 days' view would be better.

So, at a high level, you have several ways you can understand whether advertising is costing you money or not. Armed with this, you can go on to develop strategies, run tests and try to scale up. I use a combination of all the above strategies depending on my mood. This last week I've sold more books than usual for this time of year, I'm happy to make those sales but after three days of increasing numbers I looked at my ads to check I hadn't done something stupid like making an accidentally huge bid. I have over 100 books and the increase wasn't coming from just one or two books so I thought I was safe but, I have a habit of hacking my bids on my iPad at 3am.

I looked at the high level at royalties for this month and what I had spent on ads. All good. Then, because the ad spend was trending up, I dove in and sorted my individual ads by spend. I wanted to identify any ads where my spend might be blowing out. I looked at orders and ACOS and I also took a look at page reads in the dash, and estimated royalties. Everything looked fine. I pretty much know my thresholds off by heart these days so I glance at ACOS and know what's going on. I had to look one up though because I recently changed it. I am getting a lot more page reads and I decided to be less conservative. Everything was fine. I made myself a nice cup of tea, closed down my ads and got back to plotting my latest book.

Working with clusters of books in one ad or portfolio

I am a big fan of advertising more than one book with my ads. I call these 'cluster ads'. As a result, I have the complication that one ad, at the high level, is giving me information about multiple books.

In the example below we are looking inside a cluster ad I am running for some boxed sets. The book with the highest ACOS got the most impressions and sold the third highest volume of books. If we were just looking at this report and nothing else we might be tempted to switch off that book in favor of the top two books with their more sexy ACOS and higher sales – but when I look at the estimated royalties for the same period I can see that ad has helped amplify the third book. It has sold the most books and has the highest page reads. The percentage of royalties spent on ads for that book is actually less than the rest.

Active	Product	Status	Impressions	CTR	Spend	CPC	Orders	Sales	ACOS
	Total: 5		200,651	0.37%	$122.33	$0.17	83	$1,243.31	9.84%
	Box Set: The You Say Which Way	Delivering	26,245	0.68%	$29.45	$0.15	31	$476.48	6.18%
	Box Set: Three You Say Which	Delivering	34,856	0.57%	$31.30	$0.16	25	$358.15	8.74%
	Box Set: Four You Say Which Way	Delivering	123,233	0.23%	$48.47	$0.17	18	$274.13	17.68%
	Box Set: Four More You Say Which	Delivering	14,402	0.47%	$12.33	$0.18	6	$69.70	13.75%
	3 Animal Adventures: Set of Three	Delivering	1,915	0.31%	$0.78	$0.13	3	$44.85	1.74%

Full confession: that book has a couple more ads running but my point is: pulling out you ads expenditure and comparing it to your royalties for the same period for each book can be done, and is a good way to check you are heading in the right direction.

IS YOUR AD BEING NOTICED?

And is your ad being noticed by Amazon? The Click Through Rate (CTR) is the heartbeat of an ad. Impressions tell you your ad is delivering, but CTR tells you if people are taking notice. Authors who mostly make money from page reads focus on CTR rather than ACOS. I still think ACOS is worth watching, but with a higher threshold than break even. Why? Because page reads are likely following the patterns of eBook sales.

CTR is likely to be an important indicator of relevance for Amazon.

CTR is imprecise as a way to gauge profitability; CTR can be good but *still not deliver sales and page reads*. I've trialed keywords that give me a good CTR but don't result in sales. That's because my keywords aren't serving up relevance. If you have 5000 keywords over 5 ads for the same book and you rely on page reads, you will have a hard time figuring out which products and keywords make money. The way I get around this is by running smaller sets of themed keywords and products and testing what works by switching those ads off and on – do royalties go down if I pause the ads? I build up lists of effective keywords and products over time. I also read the search terms reports! Part of what I look at is CTR.

Where a keyword or category or product has a high CTR and hasn't delivered me paperback sales, it is usually because there isn't a very good match to what my book offers. However, it isn't immediately obvious to the reader and that is why I'm paying for clicks. A recent example of this came from my analysis of the middle grade category *mysteries and detectives.* I had been using this category for years for my middle grade interactive fiction books. I assumed that I was well aligned in this genre. Over a few months I saw that I got a great CTR for the category but few sales. So I have moved most of my books out of mystery and detectives.

Meanwhile my category ads have been finding me categories where my books have good CTRs and better sales. By cutting out the category *mysteries and detectives* I improved the relevance of my ads and by dropping out of the category altogether improved the relevance of my books.

There are methods and products you can look at that estimate page reads and read through for your ads. They are developed by people with good estimation skills. You could consider these products as your campaigns get more sophisticated. Then again, if you invest in creating lists that are highly relevant, you might find, like me, you don't need them. I would say don't invest too early—these products are being developed all the time and Amazon is also improving all the time. Machete is a product some people use and its website has great tips regardless of whether you use it or not. At the time of writing it offered a 30-day trial too.

Regardless, it's important to look under the hood of your ads and see which products or keywords are costing you money. (This is the second-to-last section before we look at strategies.)

DRILLING DOWN (LOOKING UNDER THE HOOD)

There are those who do very little tinkering with their ads once they are live. I am not one of those people. Here's the basic child care I do to keep my babies delivering and not overspending:

To begin with, head to the advertising dashboard and select everything in the customizable columns, just to see your options. You generally don't need all of these items at once, but they all come in handy and you can learn something from each column.

Early in an ad's life, and regularly if you make changes to bids, **sort by bid** from highest to lowest. Do this before being distracted by anything else.

Click on an ad. Click again in the (sometimes annoying) ad group. Click on the ad's targeting tab. Then click on the bid column. Sorting from highest to lowest always involves two clicks as Amazon favors lowest. (Amazon, if you are reading this, please change the default! It makes no sense.)

You **check bids first** because if an ad is spending more than you expected you might have a typo on one of your bids. I once flushed a few hundred bucks in 24 hours with a $20.00 bid that was supposed to be 20 cents. So, learn from me: don't get into ad grooming on your iPad before you get out of bed in the morning.

Next, **sort by spend**. Where is your money going? Is it logical? Is it relevant? Move your eye over to ACOS. Is it near your threshold? Is it over your threshold? Ignore this is you don't go by ACOS.

Then **look at impressions**. I have deliberately listed impressions after bid checking and spend because impressions are what people obsess on, and, while it's an important indicator, you need to check bids and spend relentlessly. Impressions generally go up if you bid higher, but not always. To some degree, it depends how *relevant* your book is to the keyword or product or category. To get an idea of relevance, look at your **Click Through Rate (CTR)**. Impressions always need to be viewed with CTR (and/or ACOS for those who can rely on ACOS without guesstimation).

Another important reason to consider impressions is to ask yourself: *Do I have an observable pattern?* The more impressions you have, the more you have to go on. Several thousand impressions is a good foundation to think you might have an observable pattern. To get several thousand impressions, you could (conservatively) wait using lower bids or throw out a bit of money with bids at the lower end of Amazon's suggested range. I usually start new word combinations well below the suggested bid range and crank them up a bit later if I'm not getting impressions. (I'm repeating myself about taking time and being a miser, I know, but I just don't like spending more than I have to.)

If the CTR is good, Amazon will generally keep delivering impressions on your ad. If it's poor, you could consider switching items off entirely or reducing the bid so that the ad isn't gearing itself to spend on an item which isn't doing well. I try and keep my ads as relevant as possible in order to deliver as cheaply as possible and keep delivering. I have a low bid (6 cents!!!) for a keyword that I know others pay more for. I get impressions. I have a 30 percent CTR. I get buys. I'm pretty sure Amazon thinks "she isn't paying us much, but we're making money from her sales and the customer is happy."

If 'book book book' has your best CTR you *can and should* do some work to come up with better keywords and product matching. Note: 'book book book' could give you your highest impressions but it's highly unlikely to give you your best return on investment.

9. Going Global – advertising in other Amazon stores

The advertising platform for other countries is a little simpler that the US. Start off by creating a simple starter ad and then bookmark the new advertising tab. You can open multiple advertising accounts at once, which I commonly do.

Start by going to your bookshelf and picking a new country to advertise in:

To change the language of the store to English just click under your name:

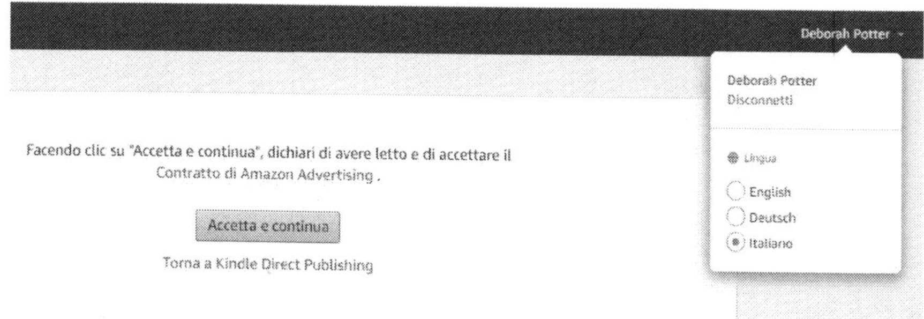

Each advertising platform requires an individual account and will generate its own bill. To get started you'll be adding a credit card to each account and there may be a ping to your account to authenticate it – my card showed a payment of €0.00 Euros.

If you need to change your card later and have any problems, try using incognito mode to make the change, this has worked for a number of problems authors have encountered as the advertising platforms expand.

You'll be used to checking your accumulating bill in the US, now you'll want to check what you owe in the new stores too. Having the stores bookmarked really helps

As with the US, billing will settle into an end of the month cycle but expect Amazon.DE and UK etc. to bill you for small amounts in the first month or so of activity to check you can pay. Now might be a good time to increase your credit limit or your debit card float!

The new stores currently only offer Sponsored Product ads without advertising copy. While this seems a lot less exciting than the US platform there is still plenty you can do.

There are words you might have in English in your metadata that have a different meaning or inference in German or Italian or French and even British English.

Some fun German examples are 'elf' which means eleven, a boot is a boat, bad is bathroom, gut is good, hell is quite a positive thing and gift means poison.

So before you run an ad in another country run your blurb and metadata through a google translator just to see what comes up.

You don't have to stress if you discover a great keyword in one country means something counter-relevant in another. Just use it as a negative keyword in your ads.

AUTOMATIC ADS IN OTHER COUNTRIES

While you may have had good results from automatic ads in the US you cannot assume the same results in other counties. This is because there is less history to refer to and won't refer to you other. You'll want to be running good optimized ads and then bring in auto ads.

I started an automatic ad in the UK in October 2018 for one of my best sellers. It ran terribly for a few months but I left it running with a low monthly bid and it gradually got better and better. At the same time I was making ads with my learnings in the US, enthusiastically reading the analytical reports and optimizing.

One of my theories about why my auto ads in the UK have performed better than the US is that the categories are cleaner. Authors haven't been stuffing their books into places they don't really belong.

I stated some automatic ads in Germany to test whether they performed like the UK. I pick the option for **dynamic bids – down only** because this is what Amazon recommends when you first start an ad. Later, when there's more sales history, you can change the bidding strategy. My German auto ads were terrible and just bled money. My sales in Germany aren't great so I turned the auto ads right down and concentrated on targeting books like mine, English only. I also added the word 'English' to my best key word descriptors. I started selling books. I unpaused my auto ads and watched money bleed away again. I am still growing the German market and I'm practicing patience.

I met with a representative from Amazon advertising last November at the 20Booksto50k convention in Vegas. I fired questions at them for half an hour. I started with information about Auto ads. I thought they'd gotten better. Amazon confirmed they had been working on them and that they sourced better market information now. They confirmed that they used customer search terms and also boughts and information from live ads to run the auto ads. Importantly though, the market information is store specific. This explains why my auto ads did so abysmally in Germany, I needed to build up some market information.

In other countries (apart from the UK) I always target by close match and lower my other bids for other types of matching.

WAIT, I'M RUNNING ADS WITH NO AD COPY????

While you don't have to provide ad copy for US ads, I had always thought it was best practice and have spent months testing and refining different hooks. So when I started advertising without copy, particularly for my children's books, I was worried.

In the US I had found I did better with ads that were very clear about the reading age. I did know though, that ad copy doesn't show up everywhere.

I discovered that advertising copy wasn't required in the UK to sell books.

One of my mentors had told me to cut my ad copy to a minimum because "first you give them a reason to buy, but the more you run on, the more reasons you give them not to buy." So I'd been playing with short copy anyway. The no copy ads did so well in the UK I started dropping copy in the US.

A book ad without copy has to stand up well with its cover. Does your cover follow the codified genre rules that tell readers what it is? If not, why not? If you can't answer this question you're probably in trouble, but if you aren't sure ask. Show people your cover and get them to guess what sort of book it is. Ask them what other books are 'like' this book. If your book doesn't pass the test, check you have quizzed people who actually read books and know a bit about genres. If they do, you might want to invest in a new cover rather than ads.

When we run ads without copy it is even more important to place that ad in relevant places. In the UK and Germany you'll want to target your advertising more closely. Your cover gives the reader a message and the placement of the ad is a second message. It says "I belong with these other books." If you get that targeting wrong and you don't belong, you'll pay for clicks that don't convert to buys or page reads and your ads won't seem relevant to Amazon.

Two Market Case Studies (DE and UK)

Germany

The German written culture has produced vast libraries of literature and genre fiction. We have Johannes Gutenberg to thank for the printing press, and it was in Germany that the mass production of books began, starting with a massive roll out of bibles.

The Germans pretty much invented the book launch and the book expo. The paperback also got its start in Germany, promptly picked up by Penguin in the UK. The Frankfurt book fair is the biggest book trade event of the year. It has thousands of exhibitions and has the widest representation of publishers of any book fair. It's the place to go to get international deals. The public get to go in on day four, if you ever get a chance GO! The fair has been running for 500 years. Each year over 10,000 reporters file news articles about what goes on there. A cute prize has been running for the oddest book title of the year since 1978 (give it a Google if you want a laugh).

I know of at least one small publishing company that uses the Frankfurt book fair to identify great European titles, particularly children's picture books, and to buy the Australasian and North American rights. If the books have proven themselves in Europe they are willing to invest globally.

The German eCommerce market is the largest in Europe, so it's no accident Amazon has been building awareness there. By population, Germany is the second largest European country (after Russia) with just under 83 million residents. Half of those people are aged between 25-55 years old – old enough to have disposable income and young enough to be tech savvy online shoppers. Online shopping is on the rise in Germany, but be aware that online shoppers have high quality expectations. German consumers are known to have higher return percentages for goods (such as clothing) than other populations.

Amazon is one of the big players in online retail in Germany, alongside Otto (which American readers may not have heard of). Otto started off selling shoes online and has mushroomed from its origins as an online mail-order business with an established household name.

In 2018 I visited Austria, Switzerland and Germany to site-check for a couple of stories I was writing. Everywhere I went I saw boxes with the big Amazon smile being unloaded from delivery vehicles. I wondered if any of those boxes contained one of my books. What you think of as the 'German' market is likely to include surrounding countries like Switzerland and Austria (another 8 million people in the 25-55 online shopping demographic).

With a long history of literary innovation, coupled with Germany's investment in technology and automation, we probably shouldn't see the German Amazon market as just an add-on and I wouldn't think Amazon does either. I fully expect innovation and experimentation to come out of dot DE in the next year or so. We didn't get a replica of the US Amazon ads platform.We likely got the start of a new direction.

THE UNITED KINGDOM

The UK has a population of 67 million, and is considered one of the most technologically savvy nations in the world. By 2021 more than 90 percent of UK internet users are expected to be shopping online. The British population is considered wealthy (by comparison to other online shopping nations) so everyone wants to sell them something. However, the UK is a smaller market than the US where one in ten retail dollars is spent online by about 200 million US shoppers.

Nearly 90 percent of UK online shoppers use Amazon and one quarter have prime membership. It isn't always a given that Amazon will be adopted wherever it opens an online store. In Australia, Amazon got huge pushback from the public (and brick and mortar book sellers) and it is only ranked the 15th most popular online source Down under.

The British do a lot of commuting by public transport and have adopted reading and listening to audio books as a common commuter activity. Famously, they are also writing while they commute, as most of the world knows thanks to P D James and her book *Fifty Shades of Grey*.

It's tempting for non-UK based authors to feel like we know the UK Amazon market. While it might be easier to browse than dot DE it is worth trying to spot the differences if you want to better understand the market. I doubled my sales when I got an Advantage account for the UK and I've kept increasing my sales over and above the effect of new books.

I got very obsessive about looking at the market alongside my books, I also read lots of reviews. Basically I was doing a more intentional survey of my little islands of the Amazon UK market than the gradual buildup of knowledge I acquired in the US. I now sell more books every day in the UK than I do in the US despite the bigger size of the US market. In part this is because my middle-grade books are likely better suited to UK tastes. When I could get ads in front of readers, I could wave and say hello come read me!

I do not have the same patterns of sales in the US and the UK. Books that don't sell as well in the US are front-runners in the UK. Books that have done well in the US don't always translate well to the UK, particularly non-fiction. I think this is because I've really had American readers in mind when preparing my non-fiction work.

EXPLORING THE NEW MARKETS

Start by going to look at your best seller. You'll want to see the also-boughts because those are books you'll want to target. If you can't see them, try changing the zip code for your delivery address or use incognito mode. If you don't have also-boughts just look at also-boughts for books like yours.

Next, look at your main categories. You are likely to see a very different top 100 line up. Many English language books appear in top 100 lists depending on the category. Europeans are not monolingual and many read in multiple languages. So while you might have thought you wouldn't stand a chance in Amazon Germany or France, you might be surprised.

You'll find new-to-you established authors humming away on other store sites too. Most of these authors, while being household names in their own country, aren't known in North America. Those authors you find in your categories might be worth researching. Their work will be setting the standard for reader expectations. If these authors are a good match for your books they might prove better targets for your ads than those you've worked to show up next to in the US.

COVERS, TITLES AND SPELLING

Take a look at the covers of books that are selling well in your genre. Some countries have different color preferences (that would be 'colour' in British English) and, while this is especially evident in children's books, I see cultural cover differences in other types of cover design too.

Early on, when publishing my first middle grade series, I received a bad revue from an American reader because of my use of British spelling. My market at that time was 80 percent American and so I switched to American spelling. These days I sell more books in the UK and I might have stuck with British English if I'd had a crystal ball. This will not likely be an issue for writers with 'grown up' readers as most non-American readers are used to American terms and spelling conventions. I think I'm actually starting to prefer American English because the z gets out a lot more often which must be nice for it. Some picture-book authors I know produce American English and British English versions of their books, it's something to consider.

Researching Keywords for New Stores

Check which languages and countries search term generators are sourcing from. Some offer quite a lot of refinement; you can choose languages, country specific searches, and platforms. Platforms can offer interesting cultural variance since social media preferences and shopping and searching habits vary globally.

Look at the reviews in your new countries – not just your own reviews but those of other authors with books like yours. Look to see how readers in England and Europe describe the books. Use those terms as keywords. Look at the blurbs of the books in the top 100, in English. You can also try blogs and publishing sites about your genre.

10. Strategies to scale up

AUTOMATIC ADS

Automatic ads gather intelligence about your book to do their thing. They use the metadata on your page, the keywords you entered when you published the book, the categories you belong to, organic sales search info, also-boughts and, importantly, the analytics from the ads you run. This last factor, advertising data, has a lot of weight.

Amazon suggests the automatic option is good for "when you are first getting started or want to launch a campaign quickly." I totally disagree with this advice. Run some manual ads for a while using logical targets and then get an auto ad going. My experience is that the auto ads will draw from my own ads and take what works. So be aware that the relevance and performance of some of your best ads may suffer if you give too much power (budget and bid settings) to automatic ads. Amazon will tend to favor the auto ad over your own ads so in the beginning it helps to give an auto ad a lower budget while it learns.

If you monitor your auto ad you can improve it over time and this is where the Auto ad can become a really efficient earner alongside your other ads.

Auto ads are not an easy set and forget option, they need training. I know that's counterintuitive for something 'automatic'. You can help an auto ad by feeding in negative targets and keywords. Use the analytics to help you do this. If you are advertising a first in series you could negative your second and third etc.

I bid higher for 'close' matches and less for the other matches. Everything I've observed from running ads tells me that readers are picking between books that offer more of what they like. I don't know how the auto ad determines a close match but that is where I want to put my money.

There are some books that auto ads won't work as well for:

- Books which have had frequent free days which built random associations
- Books which are spread over a large number of categories which really make no sense other than perhaps getting a best seller banner. This morning I saw a picture book about a shark in children's military history with the #1 best seller banner. My guess is that an auto ad would have a hard few months figuring out what to target for that book.
- Very niche books which don't easily fit within their categories – this book is a good example

AMPLIFICATION ACTIVITIES

Amplification is the effect you want to get from running successful ads. If you do well with your ads you will rank better, start showing up next to more popular books and get more organic sales. *When this happens,* which may not be a permanent effect, you can relax the purse strings on your ads. When I do this I don't crank up all my bids, I limit it for targets I think are associated with the amplification.

BAIT AND SWITCH

Sometimes I do a bait and switch tactic, I'll increase my bid for a popular title for a few hours that I already know I can get a good CTR on and then drop it back down. I'm trying to get those impressions just as cheaply when the bid drops – if I get that effect the bid is seen as being relevant and as long as I can maintain the CTR. This is a RISKY strategy. Use it when you really really know what you are doing because the reporting will lag on this strategy.

CATEGORY TESTING

You don't have to be in a category to advertise in it. Mostly. So test sales with category ads to work out the best fit. I like to run a highly targeted ad that has high relevance, and a testing ad to fish for relevance. So as I find a category that performs well in the fishing ad, I pause it there and add it to the one I want to be a high performer.

STAIR CASING

When you start out, nobody knows your name. And it is just possible the first few books you publish could be a little better, even though you spent $10 on fiver for proofing and editing. So maybe you don't pitch against Stephen King and Tolkien and the other top sellers just yet. Also: Amazon might not think you have the relevance to show up against the greats and will charge you accordingly. Might I suggest stair casing?

With this strategy you deliberately seek out the also-rans in your genre, the stars that you need a telescope to see because, despite their megawatt output, they're not #1 or #2 or #3 in the top 100. They are authors that make it to the Book Olympics but you don't hear their anthem played at the end of the race. Yet, they got there. And the clicks on their landing pages are a lot cheaper!

Stair casing, then, is a bit like anything else in life, where you make your way up fighting for recognition against less formidable players, building your form and your budget. Stair casing is also the way to go if you are trying to jump start a book which once did well or never quite took off.

Pick the books ranked #90-100 in your categories. Consider them against your book – is there a fit? Target them. If you do well at this you'll get also-bought relationships and rise up with those that move on up to better ranking. Follow those authors (I also read them) and advertise against their new releases.

Also, don't forget the old-fashioned ways of getting noticed by collaborating with those other authors. Check out their social media profiles. You might be able to collaborate on newsletters, blog posts or collections. I am quite friendly with other authors in my genres. We recognize that 'a rising tide lifts all boats'.

ADJACENT MARKETS

An adjacent market is a readership that isn't an exact fit, but might turn out to love your work. It's a close market, but not the same thing.

To test an adjacent fiction market, you should read it, consider what it delivers to the reader, and think about what your books have in common. If you can see a bridge to your book, that's your ad copy. Tell them why there's a fit with your ad blurb. Be really clear. Remember that the cover is seen first and the ad copy is often not seen. When you pick candidates for adjacent markets, put your cover next to the other cover and consider how it might speak to a reader.

You can find adjacent markets by exploring reader search terms from your ads. I've been delighted to discover brands, series and titles that readers have searched for listed in my advertising search term reports. I assume that they have been served ads that matched their initial search and then clicked onto my book displayed on a carousel on that book's product page.

Adjacent markets work well with non-fiction. Problems come in multiples. People buying books with one problem are likely to have related problems. You might have the answers. A lot of TV ads start off by asking a question about a problem the viewer might have. Do you have an aching back? Do you find it hard to chop vegetables with your blunt knives? The reader looking at books to solve their problems is the type of person who buys books to solve problems. Clearly presenting the problem that my book solves to an adjacent market sells my books.

I think the best kinds of ads for adjacent marketing are product targeted ads using book titles and products. If you find your ad working, you might add in categories, but start with the books with the closest fit.

Sweet spots

If I sell books with a good ACOS at a bid of 9 cents a click, I can go right ahead and ramp it up to 25 cents, right? Wrong, wrong, wrong. Well, almost probably wrong.

First ask yourself: Is it a really good fit for my book/product? If it honestly makes great sense, you could try gradually bidding higher. When your bid goes up, your spread will go wider. If you are seen in more places, those places might not be a good fit for your book. Related to this, when you increase your bid you will probably need your clicks to convert at a higher rate. If you bid higher, there is more scope for your ad to go into the red.

A higher bid could tip you into a different placement ratio of your ad. For instance, moving from 30 cents to 70 cents might give you a higher ratio of placement in 'top of search'. (Never make a leap this big unless you are trying a Bait and Switch and watching closely!) That changes the reader's idea of why you've appeared. On a product page you are sending the message that you are *like* another book. At the top of the search, you are effectively saying you *are* Margaret Atwood, not that you are *like* her.

Sometimes an author might be okay about their ads being in the red. If you see a lot of organic buys (amplification) because of a better ranking, then you could offset some of what the ad costs you with the rest of your royalties. But, generally, that isn't a sustainable strategy. More impressions do not necessarily mean more orders.

The sweet spot can sometimes be found by adjusting the bid down. Adjusting a bid down and waiting to see an observable pattern is one of the easiest experiments to try.

The sweet spot now isn't likely to be the future sweet spot. From time to time, authors are prepared to bid a lot more (like Black Friday) and you can step back or join in. There also seems to be a gradual upward drift of bids. I have raised the bids on most of my lucrative keywords but I've left the rest. I don't see the point in raising my bids for anything other than a stellar keyword. For the rest I practice a high budget and low bid strategy.

HIGH BUDGET AND LOW BID

This has worked well for me. I take a curated set of keywords that I have seen bring in sales and which make sense to me as relevant. This set often contains keywords that aren't conversion gold but there has been a pattern of conversion over time. The set doesn't contain test words or random words that have nothing to do with the book. I set a relatively low bid for everything. My bids used to be about 6 cents when I started this, but now they can be 12–25 cents because really low bids don't get a lot of impressions in my categories anymore and/or I'm more sure of what I'm doing. Then I give the ad a high daily budget. That is the secret sauce.

I used to think these high+low ads worked because people with really high bids have lower daily budgets. Amazon would start with their money, spend it, then move on to mine. I'm a board gamer, and there are games I play where I use this strategy. I don't have to be the first one in to buy or sell something, as there will be cheaper opportunities coming along. I do think there is an element of this working for me, but it's not the whole story.

As I mentioned, I'm using highly curated lists. The keywords have proven relevant and I think Amazon is pretty aware of that too. So it's possible I get impressions because Amazon agrees these words sell books and they really want to serve up relevant ads.

This method hasn't worked for everyone. It could also be that your book is new and Amazon doesn't give you the breadcrumbs I get with 'proven' keywords. Some markets are really cut-throat and high bids are winning all the placement. In particular this seems to be the case with categories that have a very specific framework for the genre (e.g. lots of the romance subcategories) and practically anything that gets 'hot'. But there is nothing wrong with putting a few high budget and low bid ads out there and seeing how they do.

BLURB TESTING

Using placement information, you can run comparisons of how well ad blurbs perform between your different ads.

There is a lot written about the importance of a great blurb on your book's landing page. Before you publish, it's a good idea to read up about blurbs and get feedback on yours. Read blurbs from top-selling books in your genre and note what they deliver. Those are book blurbs that are attracting readers and selling books. Refine your book blurb the best you can and then try writing ad copy for your campaign that relates to your book blurb. It's important that there isn't dissonance between the promises of your ad copy and your actual book blurb.

To test different ad copy, I sort the results for my ads by placement and only compare between the impressions served to product pages. There is a placement tab for each ad. If you are in KDP Select, you can compare performance via click through rate. If not, you get an even clearer picture by looking at sales.

You do this by downloading advertising reports or at the ad dashboard. The ad dash can give you more results over time. I like both because I'm a nerd.

I've been interested to see that placement rates are different for different ads I'm running. That makes sense—some selections of keywords target authors and titles so it's likely they will show up on product pages, whereas other keywords favor general searches when customers use the Amazon search bar.

Ad copy is more like a tweet than a typical book blurb. You want to give the right buyer a reason to click and, perhaps, the wrong buyer a reason NOT to click. For example, many of my middle grade book ad copy states 'for readers 10–12 years' because I don't want parents clicking on an ad to find out the reading age isn't a fit. I always use setting in a thriller I advertise because some people love armchair travel and others like to be closer to home. Thrillers are very competitive (Mark Dawson will tell you this!) so I use longer strings of keywords. I get fewer impressions but cheaper clicks. Many readers have preferences about the type of characters they'd like to read about—male or female, young or old, etc. Your cover might give a lot of clues about this, but if it doesn't, try giving good clues in your ad copy.

When a reader clicks through from your ad, your book's blurb should back up whatever your ad promised. If it doesn't, it creates a dissonance and doubt about choosing your book.

The longer the ad text, the less likely your hard-won collection of review stars will register. Choose one strategic point and make clear reference to it.

PORTFOLIOS

Portfolios allow you to make handy grouped sets of ads. (Note: this is a different feature to Ad Groups) Why would you group them? Firstly, you can set a budget cap across the group of ads. That's a good safety mechanism. Next, it's a way to manage a multitude. Some people have a lot of ads.

I like to group ads for a series together in a portfolio and see their collective performance—that's a better macro view for me than the default collective performance of all campaigns. If you publish in different genres (some kids' books and some non-fiction, for example) you'll really like this feature.

I've also used portfolios for seasonal ads I've developed, and which I switch off when not needed.

If you make a portfolio, you can get a grouped advertising report in the analytics section. But I never do this. I'm really happy to take down all the data and sort it myself.

The portfolio option is currently only available for sponsored products, but these are likely to be the legacy ads authors will want to start combining anyway.

If you have co-authored books or have some sort of royalty and advertising sharing situation going on, then portfolios will make you happy. They show up in billing as a group and save you lots of time combing reports to find ad spend over a bunch of shared books. If you do share advertising, keep track of refunds that Amazon sometimes make. These can occur when an ad overspends its budget.

You can group old paused ads into a portfolio and put a cap on their spend. Throwing the old ads in one place allows you a tidier view of the functioning ads (via the portfolio view) and a lot of people seem to want a tidy view. Some people have reported zombie ads – ads that have mysteriously switched back on. This has never happened to me personally but people have said they noticed when the ad started to spend. I think it's always a good idea to trim down the budget of a paused ad but for extra insurance you can put it out to pasture in a retirement portfolio and give that portfolio a low budget.

CAMPAIGN BIDDING STRATEGY ADJUSTMENTS

Amazon ads are now peppered with opportunities to tweak your bids. You can initiate it when you create your ad and when an ad is running. Adjustment strategies are something to get into after you've come to understand which keywords and product placement work best for you. You can bid higher to be placed top of search in the placements tab. Amazon will increase your bids if it thinks you can get a top position. I only do this for tried and true keywords and products. If you use it, I suggest you do so with a highly curated ad. The person appearing in the top spot doesn't necessarily get the sale. I prefer to get to the top of search in an affordable way.

Analyze Actual Customer Search Behavior

Mine your advertising analytical reports for the search terms. Put new terms into ads and send them out to collect more data. Rinse and repeat. These terms give you ideas about adjacent markets, give you new keywords, and they tell you how customers search.

Negative Games

Use negative keywords to actively exclude authors, titles, ages, opposite concepts, and unwanted brands from your ads.

Example 1: I want to target my middle grade ads against middle grade books, not baby books. I use a host of negative keywords to reduce the possibility of my books showing up against books which are for young children and babies. Amazon say they only show ads with an age range or grade level against other ads in that range. That might be the case with product page placement but it won't help with customer searches and, unfortunately, desperate children's authors give their books very wide age ranges. I use terms like mommy, baby, puppy, potty, daddy, toddler, pacifier, etc., which aren't likely to show up in middle grade blurb text.

Example 2: You write horror and you don't ever get a sale from matching with Stephen King but you keep seeing your ad served up on the great horror writer's pages using your fabulous keyword subjects: scary clown book, rabid dog novel, loco dad story, etc. You want to show up for all the general enquiries for those topics (I am just making this up. I have no idea if there is a scary clown craze). In this case, you might exclude Stephen King as a negative exact keyword.

Example 3: Filter searches. For instance, if your book has a female MC, maybe filter out male MCs. If your paranormal is about goblins and not vampires, you might exclude vampires (because, just making it up here, vampire fans aren't into goblins).

Example 4: Obvious mismatches. Looking at the search term info in UK about a year ago I saw that my 'You Say Which Way' keywords had been shown to a lot of British people searching for 'three way'. Charmingly, although I don't offer *ménage a trois* stories, I still got clicks and a few buys from this. Thank you kinky Brits! I felt it wasn't good brand association though, so 'three way' is an exact negative keyword I use in the UK.

OPTIMIZING

'Optimizing' is a phrase we use to describe identifying the targets that make you money and pruning out those that don't. 'Optimizing' is also about finding a sweet spot with your bids. You don't have to be a statistician to optimize. You do need to regularly inspect the internal dynamics of your ads.

Optimizing is about creating a campaign that is highly relevant. An indicator of relevance is your CTR (click through rate). If people are clicking on your keywords, something is working. Amazon favors RELEVANCE. Relevant ads have an edge. Optimizers are all about qualifying for the relevance bonuses. These bonuses are all about getting your keywords served at discount prices and continuing to serve your ads. If it sells, it's served.

It helps to know about how Amazon works. I'm always amazed when I hear about people selling their books on Amazon yet they don't buy books from Amazon themselves. They are at a huge disadvantage not getting the customer experience. It's a bit like people who write for a 'hot' category who don't actually read that kind of book.

If you regularly buy things on Amazon, even if you don't obsessively think about it like me, you've probably got a good idea about how it works. For instance, instead of books, look at coats on Amazon. If you can, look using the incognito mode on your browser, that way you get an idea of how Amazon behaves with little information about you. It's got me pegged. When I type in 'coats' up come women's coats in my size AND for my season here in New Zealand.

If I go coat shopping incognito, I can see Amazon trying to be as helpful as possible by offering me three broad choices: men's coats, women's coats and children's coats. It's funneling. Then it offers more choices. If you and Amazon went to a kids' birthday party and played Animal, Vegetable, Mineral, Amazon's team would win. Amazon is great at honing in from broad to specific.

Your optimization method is a lot like this too—you'll start out trying broad ideas and then end up with a set of killer keywords and bff product targets.

There are two schools of thought about tinkering with keyword bids. Some people never change their bids. They want to keep their data pure. Others—I'm one of them—change bids and optimize. One of the reasons the purists would rather trash an ad and start again was that they couldn't easily keep track of changes they made. This was a pretty good argument not to optimize before December 2018, although many of us did by running parallel ads and other methods. We no longer have to bother with such a high level of testing. Now we have more analytical data we can make changes to running ads rather than setting up new ones. And we can even see recent history.

I optimize my keywords on my high performing and high budget ads about twice a month—mid and end of month. The historical reports tell me the average cost per click I'm paying, and I find that's enough of a guide for me if I need it. With Amazon ads, the target is always moving—what people are paying for bids, what Amazon will serve my ad for, and the relevance factor in the Amazon algorithm is still a little unclear. I really don't obsess too much on the history, I'm happy to tweak and move closer to the target.

BID ADJUSTMENTS BY PLACEMENT

Once you have well optimized ads and you want to get more out of them, try adjusting your bids by placement. It pays to analyze by placement before doing this to check that your best conversion is top of search. Let Amazon have a little more leeway by increasing your bid to get there. Revisit often to see how the ad is performing.

Set and Forget Ads

Sometimes you'll find yourself heading up a mountain with no WiFi to write your novel in peace and enforced solitude, or you might end up in another country with really expensive WiFi, or you lose your glasses or go temporarily blind or … well, for some reason you need to walk away from your ads. What do you do?

One solution is to switch off your ads completely. When you are new to advertising this is a very legitimate thing to do. You don't want to be relaxing on a beach worried about your ad spend.

Another solution is to create holiday ad modifications for use at certain times of year. Leave your ads ticking with moderate to low bids using only your best keywords. Turn down the budget to a low simmer. I have ads which tick along very well without me. If someone would like to offer me a cozy cabin in the woods to write in, I'd say yes. No axe murderers, pretty please. I've achieved a high degree of relevance with these ads. The rest, my experiments and the odd automatic ad, would have their daily budget severely reduced until I came back.

I have author friends who are on incredibly tight deadlines getting their next book out. They can't spend much time on their ads. Low daily budget ads are probably the safest way to go for these people. I also like low bid/high budget but this can be less effective in highly competitive genres where the rapid releasers hang out with long series and loss leader ads. If you write series and need to be in a cabin in the woods to get book five out, try setting up ads that target whale readers (see below).

Increasingly there are also services, humans and robots, who will manage your ads for you. Since I published this book I've been surprised how many people contact me and want me to manage their ads. I really think you can do this yourself! That's why I wrote the book.

If you set your ads up and forget about them completely, they will likely run down like a sad clockwork toy. That's just how it is. But you should be able to get your ads to a stage where you can get back to writing another book or enjoying the sun and sea on some tropical island.

1000 RANDOM KEYWORDS

There is a certain appeal of keyword stuffing an ad. Amazon allows 1000 keywords in an ad and they have written encouraging words about using a lot of keywords. If you are struggling to get impressions, you would think it makes sense to try adding more keywords.

Authors know that seemingly irrelevant words like 'book book book' can deliver thousands of impressions—so why try and find relevant words? With the advent of bespoke keyword generating tools there's even more reason to try the 1000 keywords ads.

What I find with these sorts of ads is that they tend to fade away. Looking inside a few, I see they often contain dozens of variations of similar keywords. If I'm right about relevance, having a lot of keywords doing the same job might stop Amazon from recognizing relevance, and this might be part of what's causing the slow-down. I'm speculating here. At any rate, people often have difficulty filtering out good keywords from these types of ads, and more often than not they create more behemoth ads. They can have millions of impressions and very little data because the information is spread so thinly.

The ability to look at analytical reports for customer search terms is a real boon for this type of strategy. It should help sort through what converts and what doesn't. Generally, though, I find the owner of 50 ads with 1000 keywords inside is not interested in detailed analysis because the job is too jolly hard.

For me, the 1000 word ad strategy is a big fail.

THE SELFIE AD

At a certain point you might consider using your own name and book titles in a 'Selfie Ad'. You can actually test your brand value these days by running your author name in an ad and viewing the (lack of) impressions day after day, week after week. Selfie ads are useful because, in theory, they should have excellent conversion. If someone looks you up to get another book, they type in your name, see your ad, click on 'buy now', and bingo, book sold. If you are regularly seeing searches for your name, it's time to celebrate, and quickly get writing another book.

Not everyone agrees with using their name or book titles in ads. They find it annoying to pay and assume that the reader missed a free search offering. I would rather get the sale. I am a big fan of the selfie ad. I am very sure I pay less than anyone else to wallpaper my books under my other books because the CTR is good.

FIND AND MARKET YOUR NICHE(S)

Even when we write to market, there will still be a special/unique appeal about our books. You can use ad blurb comparison to test which aspects of your specialness have the most appeal.

I write in a niche (interactive fiction) but even within that I'm trying to highlight what is special about my books. I'm not trying to make them seem like they don't fit the genre; quite the opposite, I'm upping the value. For instance, my interactive fiction is gender neutral, has a Great Big List of Choices, has a lot of unique stories, it's modern, it fits for kids from different families and ethnicities. So I curate ad copy to highlight the appeal and then target that market. I target using search terms (through keyword ads) and with product placement.

By trying different sales points for your book, you can develop a better sense of what the unique appeals are. It's a bit like buying a refrigerator. All fridges keep a lot of stuff cold inside. Not all fridges have butter conditioners, or vegetable bins, or easy to lift out and clean shelves, or charcoal air filtering, or a pet food compartment, or low power mode when not in use for three days, or odor detector, or a scanner to tell you when your favorites are past their best before or need re-ordering. A salesperson talking fridges all day learns which features excite and appeal to people. After a while they have a filter for everyone walking up to a fridge. Amazon is like that salesperson. Fridges generally seem alike but actually have a few different interesting features that move the customer from *Shall I buy a fridge?* To *Which fridge will I buy?* Your ads are that salesperson, testing the product to see which features appeal, making the customer aware of the features that will appeal to them.

There is a lot of emphasis on branding your books like the rest of the books in your genre and writing to market. This is excellent advice. But once you've done all that, it helps to have a valuable point of difference that you can convey to your readers.

VOLUME, NEW RELEASES

I started out with the idea of writing ten books and then marketing them. I published them one by one as they were completed. That is not, it turns out, what most successful people were doing back then—they were waiting till they had a few to publish so they could 'rapid release' a book every month or so. That is a typical strategy for series writers. This strategy evolved as a way to sell books before authors could advertise their books. Rapid release takes advantage of an improved ranking when a book is first launched. New books don't have to start out at the end of the queue (#70 Million and One) as Amazon is all about what is shiny and new. Sometimes other new releases bump your book out of the 'new release' section quickly, other times you can last longer than 30 days. It's up to Amazon.

If you have volume, and evidence that you get read through, it makes sense to promote some books more than others. You can certainly promote them all, but you will likely want to pick your winners. It's logical to promote your first in series, for instance, because most readers start at number 1. It might not be too logical to promote a first book in a series and promise a second if the next book isn't ready for publication yet (this gets back to the ideas behind rapid release).

Knowing that new releases get special ranking, it's a good idea to keep an eye out to see what's new because *new books in your categories are cheaper to target* yet can have better visibility than other books.

OPTIMIZE YOUR CATEGORIES AND FREE KEYWORDS

If you find people are clicking some ad copy over others, consider using those phrases in your metadata.

If you find some keywords convert well, put those keywords in the free keywords metadata you set up when you first published the book on Amazon. Until Amazon ads came along, I had no idea which categories or keywords were selling my books. Now I know, and I've optimized my book metadata because of it. I've come out of some categories and gone into others.

RELEVANCE

No matter which way you choose to use Amazon ads, it pays to keep the goal in mind of being relevant and incorporating that into all your strategies.

The idea of relevance is sprinkled throughout Amazon instructional material. Getting started with Amazon ads you should sit down and make sure you really understand what they mean by relevance.

Unfortunately, nobody can tell you exactly what it means. I don't even think Amazon has a tight definition, but it is still something to keep in mind.

Amazon does give a few clues, for instance:

< click history plays an important role in our bidding algorithm. To win the auction, make sure your ad has a good click-through rate in addition to relevant keywords and a competitive bid.>

The above advice turned up about nine months ago. Here Amazon is saying that keywords need a good click through rate and they need to be relevant. Putting to one side that new ads don't have history, how can we ensure that ads are served? I think judicious pruning of keywords that don't convert to clicks is important to your ad's life. And what is a 'competitive bid'? I think here it means a bid that will sometimes win an auction. Amazon will give you a range. Should you pick the top end or higher? I don't think you should. I read the range as a range. I'm happy to start with lower exposure and build an idea of how effective a keyword (or product) is before I try and increase my exposure to that market.

Many online courses say that if a keyword is making sales then it is relevant regardless of ACOS. This is not what online mainstream Amazon sellers advise you to do. They'd never try a keyword like 'book book book', saying it isn't specific enough.

If a vendor is selling bar stools, they want their ads up next to other bar stools. They want to find a buyer who is thinking about buying a bar stool, who has gone to Amazon and typed in 'bar stool'. They might bid high to be one of the first bar stools the customer sees when they search, or they might come in later when the customer starts searching through different types of bar stools. They MOSTLY don't want to waste money showing up in irrelevant places, not getting buys and losing relevance points for the whole ad.

You want keywords with a high conversion rate at a cost where you make a profit.

I don't know how the Amazon ads algorithms work exactly but I imagine it's similar to other online bidding systems such as Google Ads where a 'quality score' is imputed into the decision-making to serve.

The ads system through KDP is highly automated. I've worked on big data projects most of my working life, and I know that every time we tried doing something a little complex in automated decision-making it caused pain and agony a little further down the track. Everyone ends up wanting to keep things extremely simple. So I don't expect achieving relevance is mystical or complicated. I also don't expect KDP advertising to be at all bespoke or different to the rest of the Amazon advertising machine. We can see wholesale importing of features from the platform that sells coats and soap and barstools. So I often sit back when I'm trying to puzzle out why an ad isn't working and think: what if I stop thinking about books and think if I'm selling soap or coats?

I hear authors complaining that their ads 'turn off' and I've had this happen myself. Generally, ads that have done well stay performing. So how can we make ads that perform? It helps to think a bit like Amazon when you set up your ad.

Here are some things we know:

- Amazon is really interested in a good customer experience.
- It tells us that relevance is rewarded.
- Amazon is not a charity.
- Amazon has a LOT of experience selling things online.

I once targeted middle grade sizes of socks and underwear with product placement ads for my middle grade books. I figured it would be a cool way to get mothers, in a shopping mode for their kids, to see my books for their 9–11-year-olds.

It bombed.

I asked Amazon why.

They told me it was a problem of relevance. Relevance is a bit of a blunt instrument, it seems. I thought it was a good idea to match books with the socks and underwear of potential readers, but Amazon didn't. When you shop for socks, you get to see other socks and choose between socks. After all, you came for socks.

However, a friend has a book about dressing up in costumes. There's a princess and a firewoman and so on and she put a product placement ad up on Amazon next to Halloween costumes of firemen and princesses. Her ads worked and she sold a bundle of books. Why did the algorithm let her through? I guess she had words like costume and Halloween in her metadata keywords that supported and gave credibility to the idea of relevance.

TARGET PRODUCTS

After the sock targeting fail I forgot about non-book targeting for a while, but eventually I came back to it. I got a little smarter about products that sync with my books. I get a better chance of delivery if the product I'm targeting has a low profit margin. That's because sellers who have higher profit margins will bid higher than me for a click. If they can make $20 from a sale I am just never going to get impressions. And it turns out my hunch about matching words in a blurb may be right. My friend's Halloween costume ad gave me this idea.

If you want to get some information about your also-bought products that are not books, switch your default amazon delivery address to one outside of the USA. Instead of book ads you'll currently get a generic list of products.

WRITE TO AMAZON

Communicating with Amazon staff is akin to conversing with ancient oracles or interpreting modern-day fortune cookies. Their responses are often obscure and not always right. I have found it's useful to be polite, clear and only ask one question at a time.

Before you contact Amazon you can also read their online advice and ask around in a few Facebook groups, the Amazon KDP author forum, or KBoards. If the answer can't be found, then write Amazon a polite email. I figure writing to Amazon and asking them questions will prompt them to clarify their online advice. I notice they have added more advice to authors about advertising lately, and this is fantastic.

One thing to note about the online advice: it is merged with and sometimes cut and paste from support for Amazon Advantage advertising. Advantage is the leading advertising application and Amazon Advertising for authors is a sort of cut down version. So sometimes the support is referring to a feature that isn't available (yet) in Amazon Ads.

I asked Amazon this important question early on: If I have the same keywords in two ads, will they bid against each other?

Amazon assured me they would not compete *as long as the ads were for books in my account written by the same author*. Their online support says something similar: that your bids won't compete if they are for the same 'brand'.

After I received the advice, I tested it. I always think this is important because, you know, someone reading fast who has English as a second language and doesn't normally work in the area your question was asked might not give 100 percent accurate answers. I'm 100 percent sure a repeated keyword over a couple of ads doesn't bid against itself.

The same should go for all the advice you get on Amazon advertising: test to see if it works for you.

DON'T KILL YOUR DARLINGS – PAUSE THEM

In 2016 I made an ad with appealing copy containing all my best keywords at the best bids at that time. It was a beautiful thing. Golden. It kept getting impressions and clicks and buys. Its ACOS, for well over a year, was 6 percent (remember I'm in paperbacks, so ACOS speaks the truth to me). Gradually, however, the ACOS began to rise. Gradually, it dawned on me that the ad—which had run well for over 12 months—could now be costing me money even though it still looked like it was under the GET OUT NOW threshold. That is because the averages Amazon was giving me went way back in time to the halcyon days when this ad was a super good moneymaking supreme queen. I was being silly and nostalgic to keep it going. I switched it off.

Just as ads get stale and stop delivering over time, they also start to cost more over time. I had hacked around with that ad. I ran test words with it (because it gave out so many impressions). I mucked around with bid prices. It was a big mess really. I sat down with my mate who also loves math, showed him several dated data points I had on the ad's ACOS and impressions and we inferred its current ACOS. It wasn't as bad as I feared, but the truth was I was worrying about it. When in doubt, just pause an ad. Sigh. I do still feel sentimentally attached to that ad.

The good news is—all those well performing keywords and that ad copy survived and lived again in other ads. That ad has grandchildren and great grandchildren.

When better reporting arrived, I was able to go back and analyze that ad over time. I could see those beautiful days when I had low bids and low ACOS. I could see the gradual decay of the ad's effectiveness. Luckily, I could also see in more recent times how it had done. So since then I've occasionally switched the ad back on for a couple of weeks. My main discovery is that the children of this ad do better for me.

I never archive ads but I am fine with pausing them. Sometimes it pays to simplify or start over. In the first part of this book I encouraged you to start a few experimental ads to learn the system and try stuff out. You'll learn stuff and make better ads. Those first ads may just be noise you can do without but they may be great testers .

TRY NEW THINGS

When Amazon adds new functionality, I try to be an early evaluator and adopter. I'm cautious. I don't want to lose money, but there are good advantages in getting in early. New types of ads will have less competition so you may pay less for exposure. New ads and tools tend to be designed to improve targeting, which generally also reduces your costs. I nearly always get good impressions from new types of ads, probably because of reduced competition.

TESTING FOR NEW BOOK IDEAS

These days, before writing a new book, I'll run some test keywords for themes and ideas related to its story. I'm looking to see if the concept is searched for and what the cost of impressions might be. I do this with testing ads and ads that have run out of steam. They have to be ads that would show in the right places. For instance, if I'm thinking of writing non-fiction about savings and shares, I can't use an ad for a kids' book that is restricted to kids' categories.

TARGETING WHALE READERS

A 'whale reader' is a term for someone who reads a lot, particularly series. They could be commuters filling their time on the train or bus, workers who have to wait long periods on call, retired folk, super-fast readers like my daughter who blinks in page content, parents waiting for kids and all the rest of us who love stories and wedge time for books into our lives. A whale reader buys more than one book at a time. They take a carrier to the library.

I am a whale reader. I am usually good for six or seven reviews on your series if it hooks me. When my mother moved to a retirement village an hour from where I live my first thought was excitement about all the audio books I'd listen to as I drove to visit her.

Authors have been tailoring their marketing to whale readers like me forever. Author newsletters and websites are there for the whale reader because the whale reader is always hunting out new material, stocking their kindle for a dry season, waiting on the next book of a favorite author..

Book three is a great place to communicate with the whale reader. If someone gets to book three they are a fan. That's where you ask for reviews (and please go back and review book one) that's where you'll get people genuinely interested in your new release notifications, and that's where you might consider wall papering a landing page with sponsored ads about your book. Pre-order pages are also great for attracting whale readers. They are making sure they get the new release when it launches but they'll also be open to having another book right now.

Whale readers search terms include the word 'like' e.g. 'books like Harlan Coben', 'books like A for Alibi'. I find the 'like' search terms come up less frequently (less impressions) but convert really well. Note that people will search for a book 'like' an author name, or a title, or a series name e.g. 'like Game of Thrones'.

Your selfie ad is also part of your whale reading strategy. If they liked what you offered the first time, you want them to be able to easily find related books you offer. Make sure you have author name, titles, and your series name in your selfie ad.

Whale readers are Amazon savvy. Since we know they like series, consider ways to indicate with your ads that you can deliver them a series.

You can target book three in someone else's series with your own book three, have clear signifiers on your covers that you have a series, such as brand name and number, and target your own first in series with ads for the latest book you have out. You'll also want to get a series link from Amazon.

Boom and Bust

There are times when book sales increase and people are more decisive about purchasing. You'll learn which of these relate to your books by watching your sales go up and down. When you see these patterns you can experiment with ads, bids and budgets to respond to those changing conditions.

I usually see an increase in adult fiction sales right before holiday weekends and I can up my bids a little to catch those stocking up their kindles. Parents buy books for kids just before school holidays. Sales go up when bad weather is forecast. Just after Christmas people get a lot pickier.

They still buy books but they browse longer. I reduce bids while post-holiday bank balances recover.

Your Attitude

Some people get very despondent about their ads. "I'm throwing in the towel!" "I'm cancelling all my ads!" I'm guessing you aren't one of those because you are reading this book. We all get a bit peeved sometimes. When we hit a good run of sales, we get used to it. When our ads work, we get used to it. But nothing lasts forever. You're going to have to innovate.

Just as you'll do well to keep adding books to your list of titles, you'll do well to add more ads and prune out the non-performers, optimize, try strategies, and hang in with the ads that are working. You need patience and a spirit of discovery. Try to be as scientific as you can in your approach, testing and building knowledge of what works for you. Rather than switch your ads off if you aren't doing well, turn the heat down. Turn the bids down, lower your budget and get back to writing your books for a week. When you go look at your ads later on, you might find there are sales and clicks and something to build on.

11. One hundred plus tips and tricks

Authors are busy people. You've come this far so I'm not going to waste your time. Therefore, these tips are brief and to the point.

50 GENERAL TIPS AND TRICKS

1. Start a diary of your promotion activity. Note any activity that might affect book sales—a blog post you made, a Facebook post that got shares, a witty tweet that got shared, a placement with promotional newsletters. If sales go up you want to know what was going on. It might be obvious this month, but when looking back you won't remember. Write it down.
2. Start logging successful keywords. Rank them as good, bad and unknown. At first, your criteria will be shaky but over time you will have an observable pattern and your good keywords will be more obvious.
3. Use product targeting ads to target other books. Keep a log of those you get clicks from. Read their blurbs. Try to understand the relationship of your book to those books. Change ad copy and blurb copy to enhance the connection.
4. Keep a folder with any correspondence you have with Amazon about ads for future reference.
5. Pause poor performing ads, and turn their daily bid right down, rather than terminate them. Keep watching for few days to get a full reading of what's going on.
6. It's tempting to put your book in front of books that are NOT like your book. Don't. Relevance is going to win you sustained sales and long-lived ads. Target books like yours.
7. If you can't find books like yours, perhaps write a little closer to a known market with your next book.

8. A quick way to view your active ads is to select a short time span, like the last 7 days, then sort by impressions from high to low. All the live ads should rise to the top. Then adjust your timespan out for a longer view, starting out with your current results. (Selecting Active Status, unfortunately, pulls up all your paused ads)
9. Try not to introduce too many variables in your ads if you want to test what works for you. Run test ads for testing keywords, etc., and only migrate the good ones into your superstar ads.
10. If you make ANY changes to your bids, always sort your ads by highest bid before you exit to make sure you haven't accidentally fat-fingered a huge bid by mistake.
11. Try doubling keywords ('unicorn unicorn') to appear under books which strongly match your themes.
12. Wallpaper your own landing page with sponsored ads for your own products. Don't let readers drift from your books by clicking on someone else's product.
13. Visit your ads frequently *even when you haven't made any changes* to see what's going on.
14. Use negative keywords to avoid having your ads shown next to books you don't align with.
15. Amazon isn't great at misspellings, so use them to your advantage for cheap clicks. For instance: *crim, romanc, horro,* etc. When you are proofing your own work look at the sort of typos you make and generalize that behavior to create search terms. Hint: people don't remember how to spell author names either.
16. Use keywords in another language if your book might appeal to an English-as-a-second-language customer.
17. Keep an eye on BookBub, Freebooksy, Fussy Librarian and other newsletters. Add titles with a good fit as exact keywords to surf their marketing wave.

18. Put change alerts on Amazon information pages to get updates when things change.
19. Use free search term engines to generate information about how people search.
20. Turn off your ad blocking software so you fully understand the Amazon experience (and you can see your own ads).
21. If you change your credit card, change your Amazon charging card immediately. If you miss a payment, all your ads are frozen and your account suspended.
22. Join or start a small group of authors to learn together, help write each other's blurbs, ad copy and share subscriptions to any paid resources you decide to invest in.
23. Spending large? Use a travel rewards credit card for your ads so you get air points as you go.
24. Keep your credit card or debit card in credit to avoid Amazon cancelling your ads if you go over budget.
25. Rename ads that you paused with the reason why you stopped it.
26. Group paused ads into a portfolio with a low budget.
27. Don't go it alone—join Facebook groups and get ideas from others.
28. Use alerts on threads about advertising to find out what people are talking about.
29. Try pared-down variants and built-up variants of expensive keywords (long tails).
30. Use 'customers also bought/viewed' to select books and authors to target.
31. Then investigate adjacent also-boughts and repeat.
32. Reduce your categories (where once the theory was to appear in as many categories as possible) to be as relevant as you can.
33. Use authors as negative keywords if they aren't relevant but appear in your categories.
34. Read your competitors ad text to see what works for others.

35. Develop reader personas—characters who are your readers. How would they search for books like yours? Get help from actual readers, and use their language instead of publishing jargon.
36. Start with middle range ranked books to advertise against and work your way up to expensive books (stair casing).
37. Invest your returns in better editing, proofing and covers.
38. Combine your results for the same keywords over different ads to see if they are useful with more data. Do this by pooling results from your analytical reports for the same terms.
39. Use a keyword finder tool with a country setting to find relevant words for different markets in your genre.
40. Put foreign keywords into your keyword metadata to help people find your books in countries where you can't advertise. Record the date you include them and record changes in sales to evaluate their effectiveness.
41. Remember the Spanish market in the US—test Spanish keywords with your ads.
42. Brainstorm new keywords off the back of successful keywords, add words and phrases.
43. Look for non-genre draws to your stories: the age of the MC, jobs they have, setting, time period.
44. Find the language your readers speak by reading your reviews and the reviews of books like yours. You can discover some good keywords this way. Try Goodreads too.
45. Brainstorm keywords that uniquely define your product.
46. Use your own titles and author name as keywords. Repeat.
47. Work with your competitors—you're selling books, people buy more than one.
48. Avoid running lots of ads with the SAME keywords. You won't bid against yourself but you may lose relevance.

49. Give your campaigns at least a month before you decide they aren't working. The lower your budget, the longer you should wait.
50. Give your ads meaningful names. Develop a shorthand for each book and include it in your ad name, then give an indication about the purpose of the ad and anything different about it. A Father's Day ad for a hunting book might read: FatherDGiftHunt1.

TIPS FOR NON-US STORES

1. Use foreign words in your free keywords metadata as the overseas stores draw from them too. Note when you do this and monitor any increase in sales.
2. Set up an author central bio for other countries (not all have them).
3. Consider publishing a separate title in some countries (only available in that country) so you can fully use the metadata. Note: you can't publish the same title in a store so you would have to withdraw your main title from that store.
4. Trial non-US English keywords in your US ads to pick up the small number of people searching for non-US English books and to build a set of trial words for your metadata.
5. Consider translating a short story as a low investment to trial advertising your work Germany, Italy, Spain or France.

TIPS FOR ADVANTAGE ACCOUNTS

1. Use negative keywords to restrict costly over-exposure and increase relevance because Advantage does not have the same category constraints as KDP's Amazon Advertising. Target, test, and curate. Then rinse and repeat.

2. Read and watch the wealth of free material on Amazon Advantage on YouTube.
3. Try keywords that have high search volume—you can test this in product page ads. Keywords get a 'traffic potential' column. You might not run the ad, but if you keep one in draft you can look at the traffic potential to understand the popularity of a keyword.
4. Advantage ads are approved very quickly so you need to watch for activity more regularly.
5. Use different ad types and explore what they offer.
6. Your advantage ads for the same book will compete against KDP ads so make a decision about which platform you are going to use with each book and stick to it.

TIPS FOR SERIES WRITERS

1. Target book three, four, or five, of series like yours. Readers looking at these books are actual series readers.
2. The bids for the second and third books in a series are a little cheaper. You might get fewer impressions, but these dedicated readers will want a new series soon and that's where you can help. Try a dedicated product targeting campaign.
3. Also read those books. Know if you are a good fit.
4. Weed out books that have low entry points or run a lot of free promotions. They will get weird also-boughts and are unreliable. Bid low, if at all.
5. Choose 'spread campaign evenly' when using lockscreen ads to give you more time to lower bids if needed. Series *with at least three in the series* are about the only books I think lockscreen ads work for.
6. Advertise your first in series widest. Target the rest of your series. I pitch third in series against end of series books. Why? It's proof to a series reader that you can deliver a series. I use a

group ad aiming to have several of my covers sitting below the target book kind of dancing around doing a can-can dance singing "we are your next series".

7. Consider creating adjacent shorter stories (novellas) to attract more readers, and as a standalone you can advertise alongside your first in series.
8. Use your novella to try different ad copy and different markets.
9. Series readers are the type of folk who snap up bargain pre-orders.
10. Target your own series with your preorders. Target your engaged readers.
11. Wallpaper your sponsored ads carousel with the rest of your books.
12. Have Amazon create a series link for you (I know it's obvious but not everyone does this!)
13. Look for adjacent markets and test with your first in series and standalones.
14. Reinvest in your first in series with improved editing and artwork.

TIPS FOR PROMOTING CHILDREN'S BOOKS

1. You'll mostly sell paperbacks, so your ACOS speaks the truth to you.
2. Use age ranges as negative keywords.
3. Use age-associated words (mommy, daddy, middle school, toddler, etc.) as negative keywords to avoid ad clicks from the wrong age group.
4. Use age as a keyword e.g. 8 years gift, 3-year-old bed wetting, 10-year-old bully, etc.
5. Withdraw from categories that are not a good fit to increase relevance and reduce overspend.

6. Try ad text and keywords relating to problems parents want to solve.
7. Try ad copy that highlights what the book can teach.
8. Use 'like' with *author name* or 'book title' to find readers looking for similar books.
9. Put thumbnails of your other titles on your book back cover—it's free advertising.
10. Try doubling keywords (unicorn unicorn) to appear against books with strongly matching themes.
11. High-cost keywords like 'bullying' can be reduced when you add a long tail, add extra words like 'middle school bullying', etc.
12. Get inspired by seasons. Use 'spooky' and 'scary' leading up to Halloween and consider changing a book's blurb to highlight its fit with a seasonal interest.
13. Ride the wave of other new releases by targeting those that closely align with you.
14. Look at the top ten books in countries such as England for your genre—often these are less polluted by cheap books flooding all the eBook categories regardless of relevance.
15. Beware lockscreen ads that can't be refined enough to achieve relevance.

TIPS FOR NON-FICTION BOOKS

1. Use How do I *solution-in-your-book* as keyword phrases, such as How do I save money on travel? How do I cook healthy meals? How do I make sales with Amazon ads?
2. Try What is *solution-in-your-book?* as a keyword phrase.
3. Use personal statements as keywords such as "I'm bored", "I'm old", "I'm overweight", "I hate math" for the problem your non-fiction fixes.

4. Load up on negative keywords to avoid crossing into areas where you don't fit. For instance, authors of vegan cookbooks could use all the different words for meat.
5. Experiment with exact terms using descriptions for exactly what you deliver.
6. Get your ads under bibliographies of well-known people of your readers' era.
7. Add work books, trackers or log books to complement your non-fiction. You may only sell a few of these, but they create added value and add to your real estate on the subject.
8. Look at titles similar to your book that already exist. Read the book blurbs for those titles and use the keywords you discover.
9. Try combining keywords that have high search volume; the combination can reduce the average bid considerably. You'll get less volume, but you will spend less. When you have some sales from your combos, you can use the search term reports to find out what your readers' search terms are, e.g. *sweet desserts* instead of *desserts*.
10. Use search term reports to make informed decisions about increasing your bids. For best results, pool your findings every month to create a large observable pattern by merging your spreadsheets.

TIPS FOR CO-AUTHORING

1. Use portfolios to group ads for co-authored books. You can set agreed advertising budgets and you can see the spend in billing via portfolio. You can take screenshots of a portfolio graph.
2. It's not a good idea to give multiple people access to your KDP account, so use portfolios to produce custom data that you can export and report to other authors with.

3. And you can pull off search terms relating to your portfolios! Use them to brainstorm with your co-authors.
4. If you are co-authoring, or publishing books for other authors, always have a contract in place that everyone has agreed to. My contracts have end dates so I can renegotiate aspects. This is really useful in the developing world of online publishing.

TIPS FOR CHRISTMAS ADVERTISING

1. Christmas advertising starts for me in October, I set up a few new ads and switch back on seasonal terms.
2. Traffic will gradually increase in November and so will your spend. Expect to spend more and load up your card.
3. Increase the frequency of your search term analysis.
4. Look for new trends to advertise to, unintended connections you want to negate, new products to target.
5. Get the holiday 'why' into your ad copy blurbs and possibly your book blurbs. 'Post this under the tree for yourself.'
6. Not all books sell better in December, consider turning down ads for books people buy themselves. People still look at stuff they want when Christmas shopping but it isn't where the money is supposed to be going. The holidays are a tight time for many and you don't want window shoppers clicking your ads.
7. Christmas shopping stops when products can't ship on time. People are still window shopping though, so turn those ads down about the 22nd of December.
8. When Christmas sales stop, download analytics from every country you advertised in and use what you find for marketing next Christmas.
9. Christmas is a time of high amplification of what works to sell your books, gift buying goes on all year (Fathers Day, Mothers Day, birthdays) so your Christmas analytics can inform general gift giving ads during the year.

10. Remember to spend some time with family and friends over Christmas and do not be that author that gives everyone a copy of their own book.

Useful resources

I have no commercial interest in any of these tools or links, they are just things I use regularly that get the job done.

Smarturl is a good free tool to create one universal link to use in blogs, on social media and websites. The link will take potential customers to their closest Amazon store. At the time of writing, the links also worked within books, as direct Amazon links have a habit of being blocked by Apple. https://manage.smarturl.it/mng/smarturl

The kindlepreneur has a couple of free tools I like. This first one is really cool. You put in your blurb text and it crafts the html to make it look as nice as a blurb can be. You'll still have to write great words though! https://kindlepreneur.com/amazon-book-description-generator/

This second kindlepreneur tool gives you an estimate of the daily sales for a book if you put in its rank. It's probably good to recall the Desiderata when you use this tool: "If you compare yourself with others, you may become vain or bitter, for always there will be greater and lesser persons than yourself." https://kindlepreneur.com/amazon-kdp-sales-rank-calculator/

Yasiv allows you to see richer detail about other books customers have bought if they've bought your book (or another book you are researching). This is great for understanding marketing connections and advertising. http://www.yasiv.com/

Pickasin is a plugin I use to gather ASINs to drop into product targeting ads.

Level Up author marketing is one to watch. Felicia Beasley manages big indie author advertising accounts and she's a strategy queen. She's building up resources on her site. She has a Facebook group too. http://procyonenterprises.com/level-up-author-marketing/

Feel free to drop in and say Hi in the Facebook ads group I hang out in: ams/aa keyword optimization - author support I go by the name of Deb Zeb. I'd love to hear what you found useful, what you disagree with, and anything you think I need to expand on.

Thank you so much to my incredible beta reading team: Melinda, Karen, Blair, Kevin, Jennifer, Susan, Bex and Melanie! Don't blame them for errors though, they are all mine.

Lastly, if you found this book useful, do me a favor and please leave a review on Amazon.

Thank you for your tme!

Deb,

January 2020.

NOTES

NOTES

NOTES

Made in the USA
San Bernardino, CA
06 March 2020